OECD Studies on Water

Improving Economic Instruments for Water Resources Management in the Republic of Buryatia (Lake Baikal Basin)

OECD
BETTER POLICIES FOR BETTER LIVES

Please cite this publication as:
OECD (2016), *Improving Economic Instruments for Water Resources Management in the Republic of Buryatia (Lake Baikal Basin)*, OECD Studies on Water, OECD Publishing, Paris.
http://dx.doi.org/10.1787/9789264266452-en

ISBN 978-92-64-26629-2 (print)
ISBN 978-92-64-26645-2 (PDF)

Series: OECD Studies on Water
ISSN 2224-5073 (print)
ISSN 2224-5081 (online)

Photo credits: Cover © Martoussevitch Alexandre

Corrigenda to OECD publications may be found on line at: *www.oecd.org/about/publishing/corrigenda.htm*.

Foreword

The present project was implemented by the OECD Task Force for the Implementation of the Environmental Action Programme for Central and Eastern Europe (EAP Task Force) with financial assistance of the European Union (General Directorate for Development and Co-operation (Devco) of the European Commission (EC)). It was implemented in close co-operation with the *"Baikal project"* co-sponsored by the Government of the Russian Federation (RF), the Global Environment Facility (GEF) and the United Nations Development Programme (UNDP). This support and co-operation are gratefully acknowledged.

The OECD contracted a group of international and local consultants to implement the project from December 2013 through March 2015. This third report, the final one for the project, was led by L.V. Pertsov, Deputy Director of Urban Economy Department (the Institute for Urban Economics/IUE). The report was co-authored by T.B. Bardakhanov, D.Sc. Economics, S.N. Ayusheyeva and Z.S. Goryunova (Baikal Institute of Nature Management, Siberian Branch of the Russian Academy of Sciences), Dr. Ben Groom and Prof. Phoebe Koundouri, experts of the London School of Economics, V.Yu. Prokofiev, Cand. Sc. (Engineering), I.V. Kolesnikov, Cand. Sc. (Engineering), IUE, S.G. Sanzhiyeva and an independent consultant, A.A. Terentyev, the Institute for Natural Resources Economics and Environmental Policy of the National Research University "Higher School of Economics". T.B. Lykova, IUE, compiled and edited the report.

The authors of draft recommendations acknowledge the contribution of officials of the Government of the Republic of Buryatia, as well as that of representatives of public authority and experts, to preparing the report. Special thanks go to T.G. Dumnova, Minister of Economy of the Republic of Buryatia, Cand. Sc. Economics; Yu.P. Safyanov, Minister of Natural Resources of the Republic of Buryatia; A.V. Lbov, First Deputy Minister of Natural Resources of the Republic of Buryatia; M.M. Fyodorov, Deputy Minister of Natural Resources of the Republic of Buryatia; O.A. Bazarova, Head of the Department for Regulation of Water Use and Water Management System with the Ministry of Nature Resources of the Republic of Buryatia; N.A. Fedoseyeva, Head of the Investment Policy Department in the Ministry of Economy of the Republic of Buryatia; and Ye.I. Makoveyeva, Senior Specialist-Expert of the Department for Regulation of Water Use and Water Management System in the Ministry of Natural Resources of the Republic of Buryatia.

The authors also express their gratitude to S.V. Kudelya, Cand. Sc. (Engineering), Director of the *"Baikal Project"* co-sponsored by the Global Environment Facility and the United Nations Development Programme, and A.A. Shekhovtzov, National Technical Director of the same *"Baikal Project"*, for their co-operation and contributions. Some data used to draft the report were submitted by bodies and organisations of the Republic of Buryatia, upon request of the Ministry of Natural Resources of the Republic of Buryatia and the group of consultants. The consultants, therefore, shall not be responsible for the accuracy of these data or for possible discrepancy with any data presented by the same organisations to a third party.

Mr. Alexandre Martoussevitch (OECD) managed the project. The authors are most grateful to the OECD officers – Kumi Kitamori, Xavier Leflaive, Krzysztof Michalak, for their valuable comments and suggestions that helped improve the final report and the interim reports under the project (Reports #1 and #2). Also they thank Maria Dubois, assistant, Lupita Johanson, communication officer (all OECD), as well as Matthew Griffiths (OECD), Mark Foss, copy-editor, and Mr. Peter Vogelpoel, typesetter, for their valuable contribution to preparing publication of the report.

The views presented in this report are those of the authors and can in no way be taken to reflect the official opinion of the governments of the Russian Federation or Republic of Buryatia, the European Union, or the OECD and its member countries.

Table of contents

Tables

Box

Acronyms and abbreviations

BAT	best available technology (or technique)
BNA	Baikal Natural Area
BOD	Biochemical oxygen demand
CEZ	Central environmental zone
COD	Chemical oxygen demand
Commission	Inter-Agency Commission for Conservation of Lake Baikal
IWRM	Integrated Water Resources Management
EAP Task Force	Environmental Action Programme Task Force in Eastern Europe, Caucasus and Central Asia
EECCA	Eastern Europe, the Caucasus and Central Asia
EID	Environmental Information Disclosure
EU	European Union
FPI "*Buryatmelioratsiya*"	Federal Public Institution "Department for Land Melioration and Water Supply for Agricultural Purposes in the Republic of Buryatia"
FTP/RTP	Federal/regional target programme
GEF	Global Environment Facility
GEF/UNDP Project Report	"Review of the current scheme for cost control and incentives to enhance economic efficiency and performance effectiveness of organisations of the water sector within the Russian part of Lake Baikal basin, with regard to the infrastructure of irrigation, water supply and sanitation. Development of recommendations for improving the system of cost control and strengthening the aforesaid incentives in these sectors", Report for GEF/UNDP project, Ulan-Ude, 2014.
GRP	Gross regional product
HES	Hydroelectric power station
HUS	Housing and utilities sector
IACG	Inter-Agency Co-ordinating Group
MAC	Maximum allowable concentration
MAELV	Maximum allowable emission limit value

Minprirody of Russian Federation
Ministry of Natural Resources and Environment of the RF

Minselkhoz of Russian Federation
Ministry of Agriculture of the RF

OECD Organisation for Economic Co-operation and Development

PES Payment for ecosystem services

RAS Russian Academy of Sciences

RB The Republic of Buryatia

R&D Research and development

RF Russian Federation

(Interim) Report #1 and (interim) Report #2
Interim reports summarising the first and second stages of the project:

Report #1: OECD EAP Task Force (2014), *Review of the implementation of economic instruments for water management in the Republic of Buryatia* (Interim Report #1), OECD, Paris, www.oecd.org/env/outreach/REPORT_2%20Economic%20Instruments%20for%20water%20management%20in%20the%20Republic%20of%20Buryatia.pdf.

Report #2: OECD EAP Task Force (2015), *Assessing and evaluating opportunities for (potentially) more efficient alternatives* (Interim Report #2), OECD, Paris, www.oecd.org/env/outreach/REPORT_1%20Economic%20Instruments%20for%20water%20management%20in%20the%20Republic%20of%20Buryatia.pdf.

2013 report OECD (2013), *Economic Instruments for Water Resources Management in the Russian Federation,* OECD, Paris, www.oecd.org/env/outreach/EIs%20for%20WRM%20in%20Russia_English_Final%20web.pdf

RIA Regulatory impact assessment

Rosgydromet Russian Federal Service for Hydrometeorology and Monitoring of the Environment

Rosprirodnadzor
Russian Federal Service for Supervising Environmental Management

Rosstat Russian Federal Service for Statistics

SC State corporation

SCUCWB Scheme of comprehensive use and conservation of water objects

SEM of Lake Baikal
State environmental monitoring of the ecosystem of Lake Baikal

SFD Siberian Federal District

MAELVs Maximum allowable emission limit values (Limits/standards for maximum allowable discharges into water objects)

SMAI Standards for maximum allowable impacts (Limits for maximum allowable negative impacts on the ecosystem of Lake Baikal)

SNiP	Construction norms and rules
SPNA	Specially protected natural areas
UN	United Nations
UNDP	United Nations Development Programme
UNESCO	United Nations Educational, Scientific and Cultural Organization
WHO	World Health Organization
WRM	Water Resources Management
WSS	Water Supply and Sanitation

Euro exchange rate as of the date of preparation of the report was RUB 64 per EUR 1.

For definitions of the basic terms used in this report see the **Glossary** (Annex D).

Executive summary

A key challenge for the Republic of Buryatia (RB), a subject of the Russian Federation (RF), is to find a right balance between environmental considerations and the need for dynamic and sustainable socio-economic development, taking into account that a major part of its territory is in Lake Baikal basin. Lake Baikal is a unique water object and ecosystem included in the UNESCO list of World Natural Heritage Areas offering significant opportunities for developing a tourism and recreation complex and some environment-oriented activities. However, it also implies strict constraints to protect Lake Baikal and Baikal Natural Area (BNA) from the negative impact of man-made, production-induced and natural factors.

The OECD project, implemented on request from the government of Buryatia, aimed to elaborate recommendations for streamlining use of economic and other instruments for water resources management (WRM). Ultimately, it sought to ensure sustainable development of the water sector, as well as socio-economic development of the RB overall.

Recommendations for Buryatia fall into the following sections:

1. Streamlining the system of goal setting and natural resources management in BNA

There is a discrepancy with respect to setting objectives and tasks within the framework of federal and regional policies. Federal documents pursue foremost the objective of protecting the Baikal Lake's ecosystems from the negative impact of man-made, production-induced and natural factors, while the RB's authorities have to ensure a balance between protecting Lake Baikal and BNA and promoting sustainable socio-economic development of Buryatia.

The process of setting the objectives of federal and regional policies requires improvement. To that end, a set of measures has been suggested:

- Streamline the system of goal setting and natural resources management in the BNA.
- Improve the information base for WRM through development of accounting, reporting and statistics in the water sector in Russia.
- Streamline system for monitoring the status of the BNA's ecosystem and create a system of compulsory information disclosure by facilities located in the BNA concerning environmental performance indicators.

2. Improvement of instruments for sustainable use and conservation of water resources

The instruments to protect water resources from overuse, from point source and diffuse pollution include: payments for water as a natural resource; charges for discharge of pollutants; taxation of individual products that contribute considerably to diffuse pollution of water resources; and proper management of production and consumption wastes in the BNA, which suffers from littering and leachates from dump sites. The recommendations focus on the following measures:

- Optimise water abstraction charge rates and improve procedures for charging and collection of payments for adverse impact on the environment.
- Establish limits for discharges of certain hazardous substances into water objects and progressively develop markets of trade in quotas for discharges.
- Introduce charge (tax) on toxic agricultural chemicals and synthetic detergents.
- Upgrade the waste management system in the BNA and promote safe management of environmentally damaging products.

3. Development of instruments for facilitating higher capitalisation of the BNA

If capitalisation of the BNA's natural potential is not enhanced, it will not be possible to ensure enough revenue and financial flows for proper protection of water resources. Nor will it be possible for maintenance, timely rehabilitation and development of the water infrastructure, as well as for mitigation of consequences of imposing limits on economic activities within the BNA. In this regard, respective set of measures was designed, including:

- Evaluate natural capital of the Baikal ecosystem and introduce payment for ecosystem services.
- Harmonise system of environmental regulation in the BNA and soften existing administrative bans on economic activities in the BNA along with a wider use of economic instruments, including state support to environment-oriented activities.
- Introduce a mechanism of compensation for environmental damage caused to the Baikal ecosystem and to the economy of coastal districts in connection with the operation of the Angara cascade of hydro-electric stations by redistributing a proportion of hydro-energy rent appropriated by operators of the cascade and by the public budget of Irkutsk Oblast.

4. Enhancement of instruments for improving the efficiency of the WSS and irrigation systems

Sustainable operation of water infrastructure requires full recovery of direct operating costs, capital costs, and resource costs. With this in mind, the report recommends to streamline tariff policy in water supply and sanitation (WSS); and facilitate introduction of charges for irrigation water as a natural resource.

5. Enhancement of system of state support to water sector and raising its cost-effectiveness

The following measures are recommended:

- Facilitate implementation of pollution treatment technologies to enable the attainment of standards for quality of water objects located within the BNA.

- Support development of urban storm water collector drainage systems and the reduction and clean-up of discharges of liquid domestic waste into Lake Baikal.

The most ambitious proposal envisages establishing a dedicated fund for support to the BNA in the form of a state corporation with its own revenue sources and spending responsibilities.

6. Improving instruments for managing risks associated with water resources

Recommendations for management of water-related risks envisage the following measures:

- Strengthen supervision for compliance with the ban on new construction projects within territories exposed to extremely high risk of water-related hazards such as mud-flows and floods.
- Introduce compulsory insurance against noncritical risks for water resources and related ecosystems; and promote compulsory insurance against the risk of water-related hazards in the BNA.
- Differentiate land tax and property tax rates, accounting for availability of infrastructure for protection from water-related hazards.

Key factors critical for implementing the recommendations

For implementation of the proposed recommendations, the following factors would be essential:

- "Political will" and good co-operation: between the levels of state governance system and with influential stakeholders with significant lobbying capabilities (e.g. energy sector), environmental and civil society organisations.
- Legislative: The centralised legal regulation in Russia means that many federal legal acts must be amended before the recommended measures can be implemented.
- Economic and financial: the RB's authorities cannot provide for full-scale maintenance and rehabilitation of water infrastructure without financial support from the RF.
- Mismatch between the boundaries of the RB and the BNA.
- Information and knowledge gaps: information for decision-making and control in regard to the ecosystem of Lake Baikal is scarce; special scientific research should be conducted before implementing some of the recommendations.

Part I

Project overview and key findings of interim reports

Part 1 of the report briefly presents methodology of this project and an overview of key findings of interim reports 1 and 2 produced under it, upon which key recommendations of this report are based (see Part II).

Furthermore it outlines policy dialogue process at sub-sovereign level in the Republic of Buryatia through which the project was implemented and drafts are of the interim and this final reports as well as recommendations were discusses and generally approved.

Chapter 1

Project overview and methodology: The role of policy dialogue

This chapter briefly outlines project background and objectives, project methodology and constraints, scope and stages, key outputs and outcomes, as well as the role of policy dialogue conducted in Buryatia at sub-sovereign level. Finally, the structure of this report is presented.

1.1. Project background

The Ministry of Natural Resources of the Republic of Buryatia (RB) asked the OECD/EAP Task Force for help to improve the use of economic instruments for water resources management (WRM) as one mechanism to achieve this sought-after balance between environmental considerations and the need for dynamic and sustainable socio-economic development of Buryatia (letter of the Minister of Natural Resources of Buryatia to the OECD EAP Task Force # 08-U031-2108 dated 13 September 2012).

Upon a positive response from the OECD, a joint ordinance of the Minister of Natural Resources of the RB and the Minister of Economy of the RB set up the **Inter-Agency Co-ordinating Group** (IACG). This group supervised implementation of the project and provided the platform for **policy dialogue** on the topic conducted at sub-sovereign level. The IACG held three policy dialogue meetings to discuss intermediate and final reports and outcomes (see Annex C).

Prior to that, in September-December 2012, the OECD reviewed economic instruments for water resources management in the Russian Federation (OECD, 2013a) hereinafter referred to as the *2013 report*.[1] Inter alia, the 2013 report reviewed the application of instruments in the Republic of Buryatia. The research helped identify core problems in the water sector of the Russian Federation (RF), to analyse and evaluate economic instruments for water resources management and to recommend how to improve water sector management through broader application of economic instruments. Its main conclusion has been: economic instruments are not well suited to fixing core problems facing the water sector of the Russian Federation; their design or implementation should be improved to manage water more effectively and efficiently, to stimulate water-use efficiency and make the best use of public funds.

Furthermore, the 2013 report states "*it would be appropriate to fine-tune, further elaborate and supplement the preliminary recommendations regarding the Republic of Buryatia, following a detailed assessment of the use of economic instruments in the water sector of the Republic, as part of Lake Baikal basin*".

The present project was aimed at implementing the above recommendation. The project has been implemented in close co-operation with, and benefited from, in-kind contributions,[2] the so-called *Baikal project* co-sponsored by the government of the Russian Federation, the Global Environment Facility (GEF) and the United Nations Development Programme (UNDP).

1.2. Objectives, methodology and constraints

The ultimate objective of OECD's project entitled "*Improving the use of economic instruments for management of water resources and water systems in the Republic of Buryatia (Lake Baikal basin)*" (hereinafter the project) was to help the Government of Buryatia to stimulate water-use efficiency, make the best use of public finance and align water security with economic and social development.

In compliance with the terms of reference (ToR), the project was carried out **in three stages**:

- Stage 1: reviewing implementation of economic instruments for water management in the Republic of Buryatia;

- Stage 2: assessing and evaluating opportunities for (potentially) more efficient and cost-effective alternatives;
- Stage 3: drafting recommendations on improving the use of economic instruments for water management in the RB.

That is Stage 1 took stock of present situation (*where we are?*), stage 2 reflected on *where do we want to be? and would how economic instruments help to get there?* While respective recommendations were developed at stage 3 so that to help implement water policy objectives.

Upon completion of each stage, respective reports were produced and discussed at policy dialogue meetings in Buryatia. The reports are as follows (see List of References at the end of this Chapter):

- Reviewing the implementation of economic instruments for water management in the Republic of Buryatia (Interim Report #1)
- Assessing and evaluating opportunities for (potentially) more efficient alternatives (Interim Report #2)
- Designing recommendations on how to improve WRM instruments in the RB (the present report, #3).

The first stage identified and documented the available economic instruments for water management. It described the way the RB uses these instruments and to what extent they appear to be useful in the context of the objectives and tasks of the water policy, and of socio-economic development of the region. With this end in view, it identified and reviewed basic instruments, and how they are applied for water management in the BNA. The instruments were assessed against the goals and objectives of socio-economic development of the RB and the BNA, as well as problems and challenges facing the water sector (water resources and water infrastructure management) within the territory. The comprehensive assessment of economic instruments for WRM, such as charges, taxes and tariffs, and various forms of state support, relied on methodology recommended by the OECD. The methodology was applied successfully in Kyrgyzstan for similar work, and in the RF for evaluation of economic instruments for WRM at the federal level (OECD, 2013a, 2013b).[3]

This approach, along with previously obtained analysis of the use of instruments for WRM in the RF, was considered within the interim report prepared at the first stage of the project (Report #1). It presented the results of the overview of the use of economic (and other) instruments for WRM in the RB, and determined the key areas of improvement for further development within the project.

The second stage reviewed opportunities for streamlining economic instruments for sound water management, and implementing them in the RB, while considering the relevant practice of the OECD and EC member states, and of the EECCA countries and other developing economies. Report #2 summarised results of this second stage. Based on the review of international practices, the report identified a number of instruments that could potentially improve water management in the RB.

Finally, the **third stage** focused on recommendations to help improve the use of economic (and other) instruments for water management by the RB government, aiming at sustainable development of the water sector, while increasing its contribution to sustainable socio-economic development of the RB.

When implementing a programme of action, the RB government relies on two factors: expected outcome and the opportunity of implementing the programme on the local ground. In this regard, special attention is given to opportunities for reforms, and to the essential aspects accompanying the reforms, particularly legislative measures and organisational arrangements. In addition, the recommendations are supported by a special assessment of compatibility between the proposed actions and the local institutional, regulatory legal framework and other factors.

The recommendations rely on the analysis and data gathered at stage 1 of the project (see Report #1). They are also informed by the analysis of whether good international practices of WRM apply in the context of the Baikal Natural Area and the RF (see Report #2 and Annex A).

The project was not aimed at elaborating detailed techniques or guidelines on how to use specific instruments. Rather, the proposed recommendations focus on streamlining water policy and on appropriate economic, administrative and information instruments that can support the project's implementation. Missing *guidelines* for implementing respective instruments for WRM might be (and should be) developed later after fundamental policy decisions are made on proposed measures.

The selected approach implies the combination of various types of instruments for efficient use and conservation of water resources, conservation of ecosystems and their biodiversity, including economic, administrative and information instruments. At the same time, it implies a sound balance of administrative constraints and economic, moral and other incentives. If potential damage for environment, economic assets and human life appears to be unacceptable, the focus should be shifted to administrative instruments (bans, constraints, standards, etc.). If potential damage is either minor, or appears to be insignificant or non-critical (e.g. when a pollutant causes no critical damage to the ecosystem, even when discharges exceed limits), the priority would be, typically, on creating incentives by means of economic (and other) instruments.

In this report, most recommendations on improving water management take into account **externalities**, including those related to the introduction of payments for ecosystem services (PES). Special consideration was given to ensuring the potential "*implementability*" of the measures in question (foremost the political acceptance, as well as technical and financial feasibility), with due account for the water sector in the BNA and in the Russian Federation at large. Chapter 9 of the present report briefly describes general factors influencing the design of the proposed recommendations and assessment of their practicability.

Most recommendations could be implemented independently; the cases of inter-related measures are specified.

The report recommends a substantial number of measures, while recognising the political acceptability for some of them appears to be low. Yet, with due regard for international practice and specificities of the BNA, the measures are designed to shape long-term and sustainable solutions with respect to the ecosystem of Lake Baikal. The authors consider the recommendations to be a kind of "strategic reserve" in the context of implementation and streamlining the instruments for water management in the BNA.

The main constraining factors that affected implementation of the project and preparation of the given report are as follows:

1. The project **has not envisaged the development of detailed methodological guidelines** on implementing or streamlining of any administrative or economic instruments for WRM. The recommendations prepared under the project, hence,

serve to address the improvement of water policy rather than development of detailed programmes, methodologies and guidelines. In the longer term, if and when positive political decisions about the proposed measures are made, the development of detailed programmes and methodologies should be considered with due attention.

2. The project was **focused on development of recommendations for the RB government**. However, the review of the water management systems in the RF and the RB confirmed that each improvement would first require amendments of the regulatory and legal framework. Practically all proposed measures require changing federal or regional law. In addition, the overwhelming majority of identified avenues of improving water management imply that **at least both federal and regional tiers of government must carry out measures together**. Regional measures (the RB) can only be implemented after being carried out at the federal level (the RF). This includes enactment of laws, and regulatory acts by the RF government and federal authorised executive bodies, including when the republic may appear as a pilot region.
3. Capacity development and data requirements for implementing the proposed measures were not specified in detail; for some instruments, this would require dedicated special research.
4. It is not possible either to propose a substantive or comprehensive solution for, or to estimate potential costs for implementation of, some recommended measures for streamlining the WRM instruments: **special applied scientific research must be conducted first**. The need for such research has been indicated in the relevant subsections of the recommendations. The most important efforts required for implementation of the recommendations are outlined in Annex B.
5. Critically, 57.1% of the BNA lies in the territory of the RB. The watershed area belonging to the RB has a decisive influence on the state of water resources and the ecosystem of Lake Baikal in general. This helped establish the boundaries of the project with the focus on WRM in the RB's part of Lake Baikal basin. The proposed recommendations could, however, apply in many cases to Irkutsk Oblast as well, which is another part of the BNA. However, this report did not undertake an "*implementability*" assessment of the proposed measures in the above-mentioned region. It does, however, specify cases where implementation of recommendations involves participation of state authorities of both the RB and Irkutsk Oblast.
6. Although up to a quarter of the water inflow into Lake Baikal is generated on the territory of Mongolia, this report has not considered issues of inter-state co-operation between the RF and Mongolia. The report only touches upon the need to develop and introduce mechanisms to co-ordinate interests between the RF and Mongolia with respect to regulation of River Selenga flow, and those concerning the development of trans-boundary co-operation on WRM. However, the project has not specifically considered these issues in any detail.

The constraints listed above should be taken into account when reading the report, analysing and implementing the recommended measures.

1.3. A brief description of key steps and the main outcome of the project

The following actions have been taken to attain the project's objectives:

- Statistical data have been collected concerning:
  - water abstraction charges and water-use charges (structure and collected revenue, water abstraction by main categories of users)
  - tariffs for water supply and sanitation and for irrigation water (level, structure, collection rates)
  - volume of water consumption according to water meters (by main user groups).
- Information has been collected on the following issues:
  - public support in relation to water management in the RB (main forms, volumes and purposes of allocated funds, allocation mechanisms, results)
  - administrative bans with respect to the environmental zones – central ("red") and buffer ("yellow") zones (capacities for compliance monitoring and enforcement).
- Affordability of water and WSS services and impact of possible tariff increase effects for water consumers have been assessed.
- The collected data have been analysed, and the water use and water resources management system in the RB has been described.
- Instruments for conservation and sustainable use of water resources in the BNA applied in the RB have been reviewed.
- International practice on the use of economic instruments for water management has been examined, including state support measures.
- Opportunities and applicability of international practice in the RB have been analysed with due account for socio-economic, institutional and natural specificities of the region.
- Recommendations on streamlining economic instruments for WRM in the RB have been formulated.

The main project deliverables: two interim reports (Reports #1 and #2) and the present final report (Report #3) – composed on the basis of the first two reports – were prepared. Main facts and conclusions presented in Reports #1 and #2 are listed hereinafter.

The main outcome of the project consists in recommendations on improving the economic instruments for WRM. These instruments were efficiently used in OECD member countries and in other economies worldwide. They may be equally valid in the RF, and notably, in the Republic of Buryatia. Specifically, they could encourage the conservation and economic use of water resources, and ensure the safety and sustainability of ecosystems in the BNA. The relevant recommendations are outlined in Section 2 of the present report.

The final report is informed by the analysis and proposals in Reports #1 and #2. The previous reports reviewed the current state of water management in the RB, detected problems relating to application of economic instruments for WRM in the RB, examined relevant international practice and identified key avenues of improving the instruments for WRM in the RB.

1.4. Policy dialogue

The **Inter-Agency Co-ordinating Group (IACG)** was set up by a joint order signed by the Minister of Natural Resources and the Minister of Economy of the RB to steer the project and provide a platform for policy dialogue on the topic. As the dialogue was conducted at sub-sovereign level, the IACG was made up of representatives of all the key agencies subordinated to the RB government and assigned with responsibilities in regard to WRM, in particular, and management of natural resources, including water, and water infrastructure, in general; as well as representatives of the relevant territorial branches of key federal agencies acting in the RB.

Representatives from the RB comprised the following:

- Ministry for Natural Resources
- Ministry of Economy
- Ministry of Agriculture and Food
- Ministry of Construction and Modernisation of Housing and Utility Sector
- Ministry for Development of Transport, Energy and Public Roads Management
- Tariff Service
- Republican Agency of Forest Management.

Representatives of the following territorial branches of key federal agencies acting in the RB were also included in the IACG:

- Department of Subsoil Use
- Department of Federal Service for Supervising Environmental Management
- Yenisei River Basin Water Department of Federal Agency for Water Resources
- Department of Federal Tax Service
- FPI "Buryatmelioratsiya".

The project's key findings and recommendations were discussed with the concerned bodies of state power in the RB. These discussions were held foremost at meetings of the Inter-Agency Co-ordinating Group. Respective policy dialogue meetings were held in January-December 2014, while the project and reports were finalised in 2015.

The IACG held three policy dialogue meetings:

1. Start-up meeting (17 April 2014): bodies of state authority of the RB decided to support the project; respective state authorities agreed to prepare the information needed for project implementation in line with a special information inquiry presented at the meeting.
2. Intermediate meeting (4 July 2014): the outcomes of the analytical stage of the project (Stage 1) and international practice in the use of WRM that might apply in the RB (Stage 2) were presented to members of the IACG and external experts. Key findings of stages 1 and 2 are presented in respective interim reports of the project (Report #1 and Report #2).
3. A conclusive meeting (19 December 2014) wrapped up the policy dialogue: project consultants presented draft recommendations to members of the IACG and external

experts; the recommendations (see Part II of this report) were discussed and generally endorsed by the IAGG.

Agenda of the IACG's meetings can be found in Annex C.

1.5. Structure of the report

The report contains a recommended programme of action, as well as steps for its implementation. The report identifies the levels (federal, regional, local) to act upon respective measures.

The body of the report encompasses two parts.

Part I briefly outlines the project's objectives and methodology. It describes, in brief, the main objectives and tasks for each stage of the project. It specifies the scope, sets out the main approaches and defines constraints that should be considered. It also summarises the main facts, findings and conclusions relating to the first two stages of the project (Interim Reports #1 and #2).

Part II presents the following recommendations on improving the management of water resources in the RB:

- Streamline the systems of policy objectives and target setting and of natural resources management in Baikal Natural Area.
- Improve instruments for sustainable use and conservation of water resources, and those of regulation and collection of payments for water as a resource.
- Develop instruments for enhancing the capitalisation of the BNA.
- Identify instruments for improving the efficiency of the WSS and irrigation systems.
- Enhance the system of state support to water sector.
- Identify instruments for managing risks associated with water resources.

The recommendations suggest the essential conditions required to implement the proposed reforms, and note the need for additional research beyond the scope of the project. Except in cases requiring special research, experts have estimated the associated costs and fiscal effect of recommendations (2014 prices). Regarding the costs of implementation of the recommended measures, only **incremental costs** (if any) are indicated in the report, i.e. costs over and above the costs of routine work of respective public authorities of the RF and RB. The estimates for incremental costs were produced based on available data on the costs of implementing similar measures and programmes in other parts of the Russian Federation. Where appropriate, costs associated with developing capacity in respective public authorities were also taken into account and estimated where possible.

Further, it briefly depicts major factors to be considered when implementing recommendations, and proposals on how to manage implementation.

Annex A lists legal acts and publications that informed analysis, Interim Reports #1 and #2 and this final report (Report #3). Annex B presents a list of additional research required for implementation of the recommendations. Finally, Annex C contains agendas of policy dialogue meetings at which key findings and recommendations of the project were discussed.

Notes

1. See OECD EAP Task Force (2013a).
2. They were provided in a report entitled "*Review of the current system of cost control and incentives to enhance economic efficiency and performance effectiveness of organisations in the irrigation and water supply and sanitation sectors within the Russian part of Lake Baikal basin. Development of recommendations for improving the system of cost control and strengthening the aforesaid incentives in these sector*s" (available only in Russian), as well as comments on the terms of reference and reports produced under this project.
3. See OECD EAP Task Force (2013a and 2013b).

References

OECD EAP Task Force (2013a), *Economic Instruments for Management of Water Resources in Russia,* OECD, Paris. www.oecd.org/env/outreach/EIs%20for%20WRM%20in%20Russia_English_Final%20web.pdf.

OECD EAP Task Force (2013b), *Improving the Use of Economic Instruments for Water Resources Management in Kyrgyzstan: the Case of Lake Issyk-Kul Basin,* OECD Publishing, Paris, www.oecd.org/environment/outreach/Kyrgyzstan_Eis%20for%20WRM_2nd%20edition_ENG%20web.pdf.

OECD EAP Task Force (2014), *Review of the implementation of economic instruments for water management in the Republic of Buryatia* (Interim Report #1), OECD, Paris, www.oecd.org/env/outreach/REPORT_2%20Economic%20Instruments%20for%20water%20management%20in%20the%20Republic%20of%20Buryatia.pdf.

OECD EAP Task Force (2015), *Assessing and evaluating opportunities for (potentially) more efficient alternatives* (Interim Report #2), OECD, Paris, www.oecd.org/env/outreach/REPORT_1%20Economic%20Instruments%20for%20water%20management%20in%20the%20Republic%20of%20Buryatia.pdf.

Chapter 2

Challenges of managing water resources and water infrastructure in the Republic of Buryatia and Lake Baikal Basin

This chapter, focuses on the challenges of managing water resources and water infrastructure in the Republic of Buryatia and Lake Baikal basin. Firstly, main facts and conclusions of the first and second interim reports of the project are presented. The findings drive the logic of presenting the recommendations in Part II of the report. The logic is explained in the final section of this chapter.

2.1. Main goals and objectives of the socio-economic development strategy, challenges and objectives of environmental protection (water) policies

The Programme for Socio-Economic Development of the Republic of Buryatia up to 2020 (approved by the RB law #1903-IV, dated 14 March 2011), identifies the following priority socio-economic sectors to be developed:

- Natural resources exploitation sector (including mining)
- Tourism-recreation sector
- Agro-industry
- Lumber industry/timber processing complex
- Innovations
- Human capacity development.

Development of the natural resources sector envisages more production of coal, uranium, gold, and start-up of zinc, lead, beryllium, molybdenum and wolfram in the republic. Major risks to water resources in the course of developing the sector are expected from possible pollution. Development of the tourism and recreation complex might imply an increase in the man-made impact on water resources in the region; this includes, in particular, an increase in both water abstraction and wastewater discharges into water objects. Growth of the RB's agricultural sector necessitates developed melioration systems due to low precipitation over the vegetation period. Development of the forest industry relies upon a high use of water and energy resources.

The federal target programme "Conservation of Lake Baikal and socio-economic development of the Baikal natural area for 2012–2020" is critically important for assuring a rational use of resources and conservation of Lake Baikal. It pursues the goal of protecting Baikal and BNA against negative effects of man-made, production-induced and natural factors.

Federal law "On Protection of Lake Baikal" regulates the legal protection framework. It recognises the lake as a "unique environmental system of the Russian Federation" and "the area of world natural heritage". The latter statement appears to be essential as the RF Constitution stipulates that international obligations have priority over national legislative requirements of the RF. The federal law "On Specially Protected Natural Areas" (#33-FZ, dated 14 March 1995), which also applies to Lake Baikal, establishes that regulatory activity takes place "for the purpose of protecting unique and typical natural systems and areas, remarkable natural formations, flora and fauna objects and their genetic stocks, exploring natural processes in biosphere, monitoring changes occurring in biosphere and raising public awareness of environmental issues".

The Water Code of the Russian Federation sets the first principle of the Russian water-use legislation and of its related regulatory legal acts. This principle says that "water objects are significant as a base of human living and activities" and as "natural resources utilised by humans for their personal and domestic needs, performance of economic and other activity, and, at the same time, an object of proprietary and other rights".

There is a contradiction between the goals and objective of republican and federal policies with respect to the use of natural resources of the BNA. Indeed, federal programmes related to the use of resources and protection of Lake Baikal seek to protect the lake and the BNA from the negative impact of man-made, production-induced and natural factors; this is in compliance with international obligations of the Russian Federation given that Lake Baikal is included on the UNESCO list of World Natural Heritage Areas. The RB, however, has to strike **a balance** between the objective of protecting Lake Baikal and the BNA from negative impacts, and the objective of promoting sustainable economic development of the republic.

2.2. The degree to which the set of instruments for management of the RB's water resources matches the goals and objectives of water policy

Review of the economic instruments for management of the RB's water resources revealed a series of discrepancies between the instruments for WRM applied in the RB, on the one hand, and the main objectives and challenges facing the republic's water sector, on the other hand. More specifically:

- Charges for water abstraction appear to be nothing but a source of replenishing the federal budget, without regard to the objectives relating to WRM in the RB. This implies that the charges fail to be an instrument for regulating volume and structure of water consumption, and do not take into account the costs of water infrastructure maintenance.
- WSS tariffs are unreasonably low, and typically do not ensure the recovery of fixed assets. There is no opportunity for covering the shortfall from public funds or some other sources, while federal decisions limit republican responsibilities in respect of designing the tariffs.
- Tariffs for supply of irrigation water are very low and are collected on a small scale. These charges are not linked to the costs for maintenance and rehabilitation of irrigation systems and effectively mismatch the objectives relating to WRM.
- Federal agencies set charges for negative impact on water objects. For that reason, when it comes to encouraging polluters to reduce their discharges, the economic situation and financial capacity of polluters in the RB are not considered.
- The amount of state funding for the water sector does not appear to be enough for even simple rehabilitation and maintenance of economic value of fixed assets of water infrastructure.
- Collection of charges for ecosystem services takes place on an extremely small scale, and has no serious influence on the state of ecosystems.

The available instruments should be considerably improved, starting with tariffs. Some other instruments not applied in the RB should be gradually introduced. Such instruments may include payment for ecosystem services, limits for discharges of certain hazardous substances into water objects, introduction of trade in pollution quotas/permits, compensation for environmental damage caused to the Lake Baikal ecosystem through hydro-electricity production, redistribution of related hydro-energy rent, taxes for diffuse pollutants, etc.

2.3. Streamlining the existing economic instruments for WRM and introducing new ones with due account for relevant practices

WRM encompasses management of both the quantity and quality of water resources. In developed countries, WRM typically relies on a comprehensive approach, and combines various instruments. Such an approach suggests consistency in selection of instruments of water use regulation at every stage of a water cycle, and due consideration of their interrelation.

Application of instruments for WRM in international practice varies significantly (see Report # 2). Primarily, there are economic instruments (for creation of positive and negative incentives, and mobilisation of funds) and administrative instruments (directive regulation), and a sound combination of the two. Information and other instruments play a secondary role, creating moral and other incentives. Over the past decades, the use of economic instruments has become more popular. At the same time, replacement of administrative instruments with economic ones may be acceptable only in cases when potential damage either occurs on a local scale, or appears to be insignificant or non-critical. Where the potential damage appears to be unacceptably high, administrative methods should be applied.

At the first stage, introduction of economic instruments for WRM in the RB envisages a wider use of payments for water as a resource (including for irrigation needs) and attainment of adequate collection rates. Almost all developed countries apply water abstraction payment in the form of water tax and water abstraction charges. The instrument helps to solve two tasks: managing the volumes and structure of water use, and mobilising the funds (including the funds relating to WRM).

When setting WSS tariffs and irrigation water tariffs, developed economies try to attain the performance indicators relating to volume and structure of water use. They also want to balance the cost of water for consumers and the financial sustainability of service providers. If it appears to be impossible or unreasonable to cover all the costs from WSS tariffs (for instance, due to limited affordability of services to residential users), public funds (state budget) should cover the difference between the costs incurred by service providers and their proceeds from collecting utility tariffs and connection fees.

An efficient instrument that balances the interests of consumers and WSS service providers involves the use of two-part tariffs that include “fixed” and “volumetric” payment components. The correctly determined two-part tariffs would encourage users to save water and, at the same time, would ensure the economic sustainability of a service provider. As a first step towards improving the tariff policy, economically reasonable tariffs should be set. These could cover operating, maintenance and capital costs, or compensate for the difference of actual tariffs and economically reasonable ones.

Taxes and charges for negative impact on water resources (pollution charges) aim to encourage polluters to reduce discharges. Substantial but adequate rates being commensurate with polluters’ financial standing would bring the maximum effect. To that end, charges may be differentiated according to a territory; time-sensitive standards, with reference to the applied production technologies, may be also established. Another efficient instrument is trade in permits (quotas) for discharge of polluting substances to water objects. Yet the scheme is not applied in the Russian Federation. For that reason, it would need to be introduced gradually. At the first stage, this mechanism can be used with respect to selected water objects and certain polluting substances.

In recent decades, many developed economies have adopted a policy for encouraging reuse of products, minimising generation of waste and waste recycling, and ensuring adequate waste management. This relates to household waste and consumption residue (waste motor oils, painting materials, expired agrochemicals, etc.). The findings included in Report #1 indicate the need for adapting the international practice and using it for reducing the pollution of water resources in the RB.

The capitalisation of the BNA is key to achieving a balance between conservation of natural resources of the Baikal’s ecosystem and attainment of sustainable economic development of the RB. To that end, it is necessary to adapt international practice for protecting biodiversity, payment for ecosystem services and support of environment-oriented activities.

Sound management of risks associated with water resources relies upon the creation of monitoring systems and introduction of measures seeking to reduce the probability of, as well as potential damage from, a risk occurrence.

Today, decisions by federal authorities appear to limit opportunities for using best practices of state support with respect to water management system of the RB. As is evident from good international practice (see Report # 2), developing support mechanisms in the water sector involves better availability of long-term loans and accumulation of the proceeds relating to water resources and the environment in specialised funds. In the context of encouraging competitive performance of agricultural producers in the RB, the continuing use of subsidies for irrigation water proves to be problematic. Such subsidies are a great deal less cost-effective than support to developing infrastructure for storage and processing of agricultural products, and creation of a system for certification of agricultural products, including export products, promotion of agricultural co-operation and others.

Findings of research into use of economic instruments for WRM in the RB, and the relevant international practice are presented in Reports #1 and #2.

2.4. The main challenges facing WRM in Buryatia and the logic of presenting the recommendations

Main problems and challenges facing the water sector in the RB

Report #1 identified a number of key unsettled issues and challenges facing the water sector in the RB, which are presented in Table 2.1. It established a correspondence between the **challenges** and **sets of measures** to address them recommended in this report.

Logic of presenting the recommendations

Since economic instruments are part of the management system, their application is not an end in itself. On the contrary, the choice of economic instruments typically depends upon achieving a primary policy goal. This means that the instruments should enable the attainment of the objectives and fulfilment of tasks of water policy and strategy as much as possible, and respond to problems and challenges facing the water sector. The instruments should interrelate and, at the same time, correlate with the water management system generally.

In this report, recommendations presented in Part II are delineated into the following thematic groups:

The first group of recommendations focuses on streamlining a system of goal setting and managing the natural resources of the RB and the BNA. They also deal with the information base for decision-making – a system of assessment and measurement that could have also been used for assessing the performance and efficiency and effectiveness of various instruments for WRM. Recommendations suggest **establishing a system of compulsory disclosure of information about environment performance indicators** relating to the facilities located in the BNA.

Table 2.1. **Crucial issues, problems and challenges facing the water sector in the RB, and possible solutions**

Issues, problems, challenges	Contributing factors	Possible solutions and recommended measures
Inconsistency of target setting and inefficient co-ordination of actions by public authorities management of the BNA, including water resources management	There are discrepancies in targets and objectives for the development of the RB and BNA set by various levels of public authorities. The vast majority of decisions with regard to the BNA are taken by federal authorities. The role of regional authorities and LSGB in making key decisions is limited, although they bear most responsibility for outcomes. Lack of co-ordination between public authorities at different levels	• Streamline the system of goal setting and of natural resources management in the BNA • Improve natural resources management administration in the RB and in the BNA • Improve the information base for WRM through development of accounting, reporting and statistics in respect of the RF's water sector • Streamline the system for monitoring the status of the BNA's ecosystem • Raise cost-effectiveness of state support to the RB water sector and to the BNA • Establish a dedicated fund for support to the BNA
The slowdown of the socio-economic development of the RB as the result of administrative restrictions and bans (not always justified) established in the BNA	The federal-level system of administrative restrictions and bans established in the BNA is not aimed at ensuring a balance between the goal of protecting Lake Baikal and BNA and the goal of sustainable economic development of the RB	• Revise water abstraction charge rates • Establish limits for discharges of certain hazardous substances into water objects and progressive development of market for quotas for discharges • Evaluate natural capital of the Baikal ecosystem • Harmonise system of environmental regulation in the BNA and mitigate administrative bans along with a wider use of economic instruments for managing activities in the central environmental zone of the BNA. • Provide state support to economic environment-oriented activities (to enhance capitalisation of the BNA) • Introduce payments for ecosystem services (PES) • Introduce a system of compulsory insurance against noncritical risks for water resources and related ecosystems and for biodiversity in the BNA
Inadequate development and high level of tear and wear of WSS systems and irrigation systems. Acute shortage of funds for rehabilitation of the water infrastructure of all types, as well as funds for elimination of the past environmental damage	Tariff revenues of the WSS sector, budget and off-budget financing for irrigation systems, hydro-technical structures and other water infrastructure do not provide a sufficient amount of funds even for the routine maintenance and rehabilitation of fixed assets in the water sector There is a steady trend of deterioration of the condition of WSS systems and irrigation systems in the RB	• Improve procedures for charging and collection of charges for pollution and other adverse impact on the environment • Establish limits for discharges of certain hazardous substances into water objects and progressive development of market for quotas for discharges • Introduce charge (tax) on toxic agricultural chemicals (pesticides, herbicides, etc.), and on synthetic detergents • Streamline tariff policy in the WSS • Facilitate introduction of charges for irrigation water as natural resource • Establish a dedicated fund for support to the BNA. • Provide state support of environment-oriented activities (to increase capitalisation of the BNA) • Introduce a mechanism of compensation for environmental damage caused to the Baikal ecosystem and to the economy of coastal districts in connection with the operation of the Angara HES cascade by redistributing a proportion of appropriated hydro-energy rent. Facilitate implementation of pollution treatment technologies to enable the attainment of standards for quality of water objects located within the BNA

Table 2.1. **Crucial issues, problems and challenges facing the water sector in the RB, and possible solutions** *(continued)*

Issues, problems, challenges	Contributing factors	Possible solutions and recommended measures
Insufficient incentives to encourage polluters to reduce discharges into water objects and implement respective environmental interventions	The applied economic and administrative management instruments provide minor incentives to polluters for reducing discharges and implementing respective environmental interventions. The available incentives are established at the federal level and can hardly take into account the economic potential of polluters in the RB	• Create a system of compulsory information disclosure concerning environmental performance indicators in respect of the facilities located in the BNA • Revise water abstraction charge rates • Improve procedures for charging and collection of charges for pollution and other adverse impact on the environment • Introduce charge (tax) on toxic agricultural chemicals (pesticides, herbicides, etc.) and on synthetic detergents • Upgrade the waste management system in the BNA, and promote safe management of environmentally damaging products • Facilitate implementation of pollution treatment technologies to enable the attainment of standards for quality of water objects located within the BNA • Support development of storm water collector drainage systems, local wastewater disposal systems, reduction and clean-up of discharges of liquid domestic waste into Lake Baikal
Diffuse pollution of water objects; littering of near-shore areas of surface water objects	The environmental situation in the BNA suffers from the absence of instruments for controlling diffuse pollution, as well as from shortcomings in the system of handling wastes, including solid and liquid domestic wastes	• Streamline the system for monitoring the status of the BNA's ecosystem • Introduce charge (tax) on toxic agricultural chemicals (pesticides, herbicides, etc.) and on synthetic detergents • Upgrade the waste management system in the BNA, and promote safe management of environmentally damaging products • Support development of storm water collector drainage systems, local wastewater disposal systems, reduction and clean-up of discharges of liquid domestic waste into Lake Baikal
Inadequate risk management for the negative impact of water-related hazards (floods, underflooding, mud-flows) in the RB territory	The system for prevention of the negative impact of water-related hazards in the RB does not foster a sufficient minimisation of the risk of floods, ground water flooding, mud-flows and/or reduction of damage from those hazards.	• Streamline the system for monitoring the status of the BNA's ecosystem • Facilitate efforts to ensure that water level fluctuations of Lake Baikal are close to their natural values • Strengthen supervision for compliance with the ban on new construction projects within the territories exposed to the extremely high risk of water-related hazards • Promote a system of compulsory insurance against the risk of water-related hazards in the BNA • Differentiate land tax rates and property tax rates, accounting for availability and quality of infrastructure for protection from water-related hazards.

Source: Authors' own assessment and proposal.

The second group of recommendations covers the conservation of water resources from their overuse, as well as protecting them from point source pollution and non-point source (diffuse) pollution. The instruments serving to tackle the tasks include payments for water as a natural resource; charges for pollution, taxes on individual types of products that contribute considerably to the non-point source pollution of water resources, and proper management of production and consumption waste in the BNA (where water resources suffer from littering, leachates from dump sites and so on).

The third group of recommendations suggests how to increase the capitalisation of the BNA through relevant instruments such as economic evaluation of natural resources, promotion of environment-oriented activities, introduction of a mechanism to compensate for environmental damage caused to the Baikal ecosystem and to the economy of coastal districts due to operations of the Angara HES cascade by redistribution of a proportion of hydro-energy rent, introduction of payments for ecosystem services and harmonisation of the system of environmental regulation in the BNA.

The fourth group of recommendations concerns the economic instruments designed to improve the efficiency and financial sustainability of water infrastructure systems, including WSS tariffs and irrigation tariffs.

The fifth group of recommendations focuses on improving the instruments of state support in regard to water management in the RB.

The sixth set of recommendations highlights the instruments used to manage water-related hazards, and the risks to water resources, as well as a mechanism of compensation for environmental damage caused as a result of a risk occurrence.

Special attention is given to common factors that should be considered when implementing the recommendations, and to proposals on how to manage implementation.

Recommendations for the RB based on analysis of data with due consideration for the relevant international practice (see Report #2) offer, in general, a balanced combination of administrative, economic and other instruments. Together, they reconcile the economic interests of the republic and the need to conserve the unique ecosystem of Lake Baikal.

References

RB law #1903-IV, dated 14 March 2011.

Government of the Russian Federation, Decree "On Federal Target Programme "Protection of Lake Baikal and Socio-Economic Development of the Baikal Natural Area in 2012-2020" (21 August 2012, #847).

Government of the Russian Federation, Federal Law "On Specially Protected Natural Areas" (14 March 1995, #33-ФЗ).

Part II

Recommendations on improving the economic instruments for water management in the Republic of Buryatia

Part II presents recommendations of the project (Chapters 3-8) followed by discussion of factors essential for implementing the recommendations and proposals on how to manage the implementation process (Chapter 9).

Chapter 3

Streamlining goal setting and natural resources management

This chapter presents recommendations on improving the overall management of natural resources in the Baikal Natural Area (BNA), including through: streamlining the policy goal-setting system; improving the information base for WRM s; creation of a system of compulsory information disclosure concerning environmental performance indicators; and streamlining the system of monitoring of the status of the BNA's ecosystem.

3.1. Streamlining the policy goal-setting system in regard to management of the BNA

Problem description

Several basic federal legislative acts regulate protection of Lake Baikal, such as the RF Constitution, the RF Water Code, the RF Urban Planning Code, the RF Water Strategy, Federal Law "On Protection of the Environment", Federal Law "On Protection of Lake Baikal" and a number of government decrees enacted in relation to these laws.

The analysis reveals a system of objectives and tasks, applied in policy documents relating to management of water resources in the BNA, that relies on different approaches. The above-mentioned federal acts stipulate that the main objective of WRM is to protect Lake Baikal and the BNA from the negative impact of man-made, production-induced and natural factors. At the same time, the RB's authorities, when determining priorities of conserving water resources and promoting their sustainable use, need to strike a balance between protecting Lake Baikal and the BNA from negative impacts, and providing for sustainable economic development of the republic. The systems of objectives and tasks in various regulatory acts relating to the BNA, hence, require revision and streamlining, as well as the goal-setting acts.

A standalone problem relates to the setting of policy objectives in respect of the BNA. It stems from the poorly defined status of a scheme of comprehensive use and conservation of water bodies (SCUCWB), as it relates to the entire system of water objects available in the BNA. In accordance with the RF Water Code, the SCUCWB encompasses and systematises all the main data about the state and use of water objects. It underlies the performance of water management and protection measures in relation to water objects located within river basins. The RF Urban Planning Code also lacks a clearly articulated definition of the status of the SCUCWB as a planning document, which appears to be a shared problem throughout the Russian Federation.

The Yenisei River Basin Water Department of the Federal Agency for Water Resources has designed a considerable part of the SCUCWB for Lake Baikal basin and approved it by the department's orders (http://skiovo.enbvu.ru/). The work has yet to be completed. There is also a need to revise current federal guidelines to ensure the design of the SCUCWB fully reflects specificity of the BNA.

Outline of measures

1. Revise the policy objectives and tasks; amend respective federal and regional regulatory acts on protection of Lake Baikal; and reconcile these acts with legislative requirements of the RF Water Code, the RF Urban Planning Code and the Federal Law "On Protection of Lake Baikal", as well as with the RF's international obligations in respect of enforcing laws and regulations to conserve the unique ecosystem of Lake Baikal.

While doing so, policy makers need to pay attention to the legal and regulatory framework as it relates to the protection of Lake Baikal as a natural area included on the list of the World Natural Heritage Areas. In addition, in regard to the setting of objectives, special attention might be paid to raising environmental awareness and cultural standards of the RB residents and tourists travelling to the BNA.

2. Define the status of the SCUCWB as a planning document in the RF Urban Planning Code to harmonise the federal legislative requirements in respect of the instrument for WRM.

3. Revise federal guidelines for designing SCUCWB, and complete the development and approve all schemes of comprehensive use and conservation of water objects available in the BNA.

Estimated incremental cost and fiscal effect

Measures 1 and 2 (see Table 3.1) could be implemented as part of the routine work of public authorities. There appear to be no direct incremental costs or influence on budget revenue. Measure 3 may cost between RUB 25-35 million (expert estimate).

Table 3.1. **"Implementability" and estimated period of implementation**

Measure	"Implementability"	Period of implementation	
		Based on the scope of work	Taking into account political, social and economic acceptability
Revising the policy objectives and tasks and amending respective federal and regional legal acts on the protection of Lake Baikal	Moderate	1-2 years	1-2 years
Defining the status of schemes of comprehensive use and conservation of water objects as a planning document incorporated into the RF Urban Planning Code	High	6 months-1 year	6 months-1 year
Revising federal guidelines for designing SCUCWB, completing the development and approving all the schemes of comprehensive use and conservation of water objects in the BNA	High	1-2 years	1-2 years

Source: Authors' recommendations and estimates.

Implementing the measures: level of authority involved and relationship with the Russian Federation's water policy

Taking into account division of responsibilities between the levels of state governance system in the RF, federal and regional authorities have the power to jointly implement Measure 1 with the aim of enhancing the efficiency of WRM in the BNA (with federal authority amending respective federal legal acts and regional authority bringing regional acts in line with federal ones). This concerns both the RB's authorities and regional authorities of Irkutsk Oblast. Responsibilities for implementation of Measures 2 and 3 are entirely assigned to federal authorities. The recommended measures may be carried out independently.

Expected outcome

- harmonised federal law on protection of Lake Baikal and protection of the BNA from negative impact of man-made, production-induced and natural factors
- a framework for streamlining the system of WRM for the BNA, and new instruments that help achieve a balance between conservation of the ecosystem of Lake Baikal and sustainable socio-economic development of the RB.

3.2. Improving natural resources management administration in the RB and in the BNA

Problem description

In recent decades, many world economies have emphasised integrated water resources management (IWRM), as well as estimating relationships between various social, economic and environmental aspects associated with water. The UN defines IWRM as "a process which promotes the co-ordinated development and management of water, land and related resources, in order to maximise the resultant economic and social welfare in an equitable manner without compromising the sustainability of vital ecosystems". Water management, administered in such a way, should result in less damage to biodiversity and natural ecosystems, and, thereby, secure the human right to a favourable environment, including to clean fresh water. This principle of water management was enacted by Resolution of the UN General Assembly issued on 29 July 2010.

Introduction of IRWM principles for Lake Baikal demands more efficient institutional mechanisms at every level (tier) of the public governance system. In addition, the relevant functions should be clearly defined in respect to each tier. Mechanisms for vertical and horizontal co-ordination of the functions between the tiers should also be designed.

The Inter-Agency Commission for Conservation of Lake Baikal (the Commission) was set up to co-ordinate the streamlining of the integrated management of water and other natural resources in the BNA in accordance with the federal law "On Protection of Lake Baikal" (#94-FZ, dated 1 May 1999). It performs the tasks outlined below:

- co-ordinating research, restoration, use and conservation of natural resources of the BNA; conserving biodiversity; promoting environmental security; implementing socio-economic tasks facing the region
- improving the regulatory framework in respect to protection of the environment and sustainable use of natural resources of the BNA
- performing the state ecological monitoring of the unique ecosystem of Lake Baikal
- fulfilling the RF's international obligations as they relate to protection of Lake Baikal as an object included on the UNESCO list of World Natural Heritage Areas.

Based on its several years of work, however, the Commission was not as inefficient as expected. The need for raising its profile is clear, along with broadening its power to perform the assigned functions.

Outline of measures

1. Raise the profile of the Inter-Agency Commission for Conservation of Lake Baikal as a body co-ordinating the policy of protection and use of natural resources in the BNA, including development of IWRM.

2. Integrate the results of the GEF/UNDP project, "The *Integrated* Natural Resources Management in the *Baikal* Basin Trans-Boundary Ecosystem", into the practice of management in respect of the BNA. This relates specifically to evaluating the potential of the basin management and implementing the programme on augmenting the potential of sub-basin management, with due consideration of comprehensive planning and mapping based on geo-information systems.

Comprehensive water resources management should be considered to help improve the system of setting policy goals for management of the BNA.

Estimated incremental cost and fiscal effect

The measures may be implemented as part of the routine work of public authorities. Direct incremental costs and direct influence on budget revenue appear to be non-existent.

Implementing the measures: level of authority and relationship with the Russian Federation's water policy

The measures outlined in Table 3.2 seek to enhance the efficiency of WRM in the BNA. Implementation requires actions by federal authorities in co-operation with regional authorities of the RB and Irkutsk Oblast. The recommended measures may be carried out independently.

Table 3.2. **"Implementability" and estimated period of implementation**

Measure	"Implementability"	Period of implementation	
		Based on the scope of work	Taking into account political, social and economic acceptability
Raising the profile of the Inter-Agency Commission for Conservation of Lake Baikal as a body co-ordinating the policy of protection and use of natural resources in the BNA, and assigning the development of IWRM to the Commission	Moderate	1 year	1 year
Integrating the results of the GEF and UNDP project "The *Integrated* Natural Resources Management in the *Baikal* Basin Trans-Boundary Ecosystem" into the practice of management in respect of the BNA as it relates to evaluating the potential of the basin management and implementing the programmes	Moderate	1-2 years	1-2 years

Source: Authors' recommendations and estimates.

Expected outcome

- Higher profile for the Inter-Agency Commission for Conservation of Lake Baikal
- Better inter-agency co-ordination on issues related to management of the BNA and increased integrity of WRM in respect of the BNA.

3.3. Improving information base for WRM: development of accounting, reporting and statistics on the Russian Federation's water sector

Problem description

Statistical accounting on the RF's water sector mainly relies on data published in annual statistical reports "On Environment Protection in Russia" issued by the Federal State Statistics Service (Rosstat), and sector statistics (including data submitted according to the reporting form *2tp-vodkhoz*). The sector statistics are summarised in "On the State and Protection of the Environment" reports prepared by regional authorities (or by federal authorities in regard to the data relating to the Russian Federation as a whole, and to BNA specifically[1]).

With regard to WSS organisations, Rosstat gathers data presented in respective exsting reporting formats (# 1-water supply, #1-sanitation, #1-utility sector, and #22-zhkh (aggregate)).

The analysis (see Report #1) detected a number of shortcomings in accounting, reporting and statistics on the RF water sector.

1. The system of statistical accounting appears to be generally sufficient in terms of the key aspects of water use and management of water resources. The Rosstat's statistics, however, contain only core indicators in respect of water use and WRM, while more detailed data are not always available. The authorities of the RF regions, at their discretion, select a template in which to prepare the regional reports "On the State of Environment and its Protection". There are no general requirements for the list of indicators and data to be covered in the reports. The actually used indicators and data presented fail to provide a systemic view of the use of water at every stage of the "water cycle" (abstraction and use of water, treatment of wastewater and discharge of wastewater into water objects by various users). In addition, the current statistical accounting is lacking data related to BNA.

2. The data on WSS collected using the above-mentioned Rosstat's statistical report formats are not readily available. In addition, data in respect of WSS appear to be somewhat distorted as outlined below:

- presentation of data about estimated "normative losses" of water in WSS networks instead of on actual losses;
- presentation of data on monitoring quality of drinking water pumped by companies into water distribution networks rather than at the boundary of the areas of responsibility of water companies and consumers (at the points of connection to residential buildings and distribution networks of organisations), that is, without considering the effects of the state (at times, the dire state) of the water supply network for the quality of water at water supply points (tap water).

3. The public budget classification in the Russian Federation does not allow attachment of expenditure items to the management of natural resources, and, specifically, water resources and development of water management systems. The classification, annually established by the Ministry of Finance, contains some items of expenditure relating to the water sector (notably, "Protection of population and territory from natural and production-induced emergency situations, and civil defence", "Water Management System", "Utilities System"). These items, however, do not encompass all water sector issues, and are not confined to the sector either.

The Russian Federation does not appear to have a uniform approach to allocation of budget expenditures towards WRM and management of natural resources at large. Indeed, expenditures for construction, rehabilitation and development of water management systems – among them also WSS networks and facilities – may be incorporated into such items of public expenditures as "National economy" (e.g. WSS infrastructure in special economic zones) and even "National defence" (e.g. WSS systems in military units and military settlements).

The above-mentioned deficiencies of classification of budget expenditures tend to be common across the Russian Federation. In the context of WRM in the RB, deficiencies result in poorly informed public authorities. This negatively affects the relevant decision-making process, as well as the quality of WRM and performance of water management system in Buryatia.

Outline of measures

1. Assign to the Rosstat the responsibility of issuing an annual statistical report on the state of the water sector and WRM and including this responsibility in the Federal Plan of Statistical Work (Decree of the RF government #671-p signed 6 May 2008). The foregoing report should be composed with due consideration for the comprehensive definition of the "water cycle" applied by the OECD.

2. Approving methodological guidelines by the Ministry of Natural Resources and Environmental Protection of the Russian Federation (*Minprirody*) for the regions of the RF in respect of preparation of reports "On the State of the Environment and its Protection". A list of recommendable indicators on the state of WRM in the regions must be included in the guidelines.

3. Adjusting the forms of statistical reporting as it relates to the WSS sector, and promoting open access to integrated data about WSS. Changes to help solve the indicated problems should be introduced in the forms of statistical reporting.

4. Approving and adjusting the methodological guidelines on classification of public budget expenditures for WRM, in particular, and expenditure for management of natural resources, on the whole, by the *Minprirody* of the Russian Federation. They should be adjusted regularly since the RF revises budget classifications regularly, and, hence, classifiers set in various years can have certain differences.

Estimated incremental cost and fiscal effect

The measures may be implemented as part of public authorities' current activity at no direct incremental costs; direct influence on budget revenue also appears to be non-existent.

Implementing the measures: level of authority and relationship with the Russian Federation's water policy

The measures (Table 3.3) are common elements of the Russian Federation's water policy. Implementation requires actions by federal authorities in the interests of data users across the entire territory of the RF.

The recommended measures may be carried out independently.

Table 3.3. **"Implementability" and estimated period of implementation**

		Period of implementation	
Measure	"Implementability"	Based on the scope of work	Taking into account political, social and economic acceptability
Including the Rosstat's responsibility of issuing an annual statistical report on the state of the water sector and WRM into the Federal Plan of Statistical Work	High	1-2 years	1-2 years
Approving methodological guidelines by the Minprirody of the Russian Federation in respect of preparation of reports "On the State of the Environment and its Protection"	High	6 months-1 year	6 months-1 year

Table 3.3. **"Implementability" and estimated period of implementation** *(continued)*

Measure	"Implementability"	Period of implementation	
		Based on the scope of work	Taking into account political, social and economic acceptability
Adjusting the forms of statistical reporting to promote open access to integrated data on WSS	Moderate*	6 months-1 year	6 months-1 year
Approving and adjusting methodological guidelines on classification of public budget expenditures for WRM and management of natural resources by the Minprirody of the Russian Federation	High	6 months-1 year	6 months-1 year

* The use of estimated "normative losses" instead of actual losses in WSS networks water in Rosstat's forms may result in inaccurate accounting of the indicator when setting the tariffs for WSS enterprises. This undermines the chances of adjusting the statistical reporting forms.

Source: Authors' recommendations and estimates.

Expected outcome

- more complete and available information relating to the state of the water sector and water management for WRM systems in Buryatia
- an opportunity for an integrated analysis of budget expenditures for water sector and WRM assigned to the levels of RF budget system.

3.4. Creation of a system of compulsory information disclosure concerning environmental performance indicators in respect of the facilities in the BNA

Problem description

In international practice, **environmental information disclosure (EID)** is an essential tool for supervision and promotion of transparency in respect of performance of organisations engaged in environmental and economic activities. The approach is hardly new in the Russian Federation. In fact, RF law obliges utility companies to publish information about their operational performance. However, special regulation of the EID on environmentally sensitive significant territories, notably in the BNA, has not yet been established.

It is recommended that the BNA – with its unique ecosystem and special environmental management regulation – be a pilot Russian site for setting the requirements for **compulsory disclosure of environmental information**. As indicated in Report #2, the relevant measures may encourage fewer discharges of hazardous substances into water objects of the BNA, and draw more public attention to problems relating to the state of Lake Baikal ecosystem.

Outline of measures

1. Develop regulatory legal framework and methodology for compulsory disclosure of environment-related information by enterprises located in the BNA, and more specifically:

- Amend Federal Law "On Protection of Lake Baikal" as it relates to provisions regulating the introduction of a system of compulsory EID for enterprises located in the BNA.

- Design a system of ratings and assign environmental status of enterprises through a breakdown by groups and types.
- Develop legal framework in respect of compulsory disclosure of information concerning environmental performance of enterprises.

With due regard to the international practice of the EID, an environmental grading system – as exemplified in Table 3.4 – might be set up to categorise the environmental performance of enterprises in the RB.

Table 3.4. **Characteristics of environmental performance of enterprises in the RB**

"Colour" labelling system	Environmental characteristics
Green	Best available technologies (BAT) is applied and ensures minimal generation of waste and pollution; treatment technology meets the highest international standards
Blue	Well above the level of standard prescribed by environmental requirements in effect in the RF
White	Up to (or slightly above) the standards prescribed by environmental requirements in effect in the RF
Red	Below the standards prescribed by environmental requirements in effect in the RF
Black	Causing serious damage to the environment when effective pollution control is practically non-existent

Source: Authors' own elaboration.

Establishing requirements to the EID necessitates relying on both the relevant international practice and considering the Russian Federation's experience in applying the EID standards in the utilities sector. In this regard, the process should start by identifying a list of easily controlled indicators. They should allow enterprises to be categorised according to their environmental performance indicators.

2. Implement a pilot project in the BNA. Possible stages of a pilot project are as follows:

- Select a pilot group of enterprises and design a monitoring procedure for the group.
- Collect and assess information received from a pilot group of enterprises.
- Extend list of enterprises to encompass all those in the BNA.
- Introduce a system of compulsory presentation of information about the environmental status and performance of enterprises or facilities, and make the information widely available.

An alternative option envisages the implementation of a pilot project either only in the RB or simultaneously in the RB and Irkutsk Oblast.

3. Organise a campaign to evaluate the results of awarding ratings to enterprises, and making the information available to mass media. The campaign should rely on the EID to identify the most environmentally advanced enterprises.

Estimated incremental cost and fiscal effect

For the most part, the measures may be implemented as part of the routine work of public authorities. There do not appear to be direct incremental costs or a direct influence on budget revenue. Developing the methodology and implementation plan may require extra research. The cost of work may be estimated at RUB 10-15 million.

Implementing the measures: level of authority and relationship with the Russian Federation's water policy

The measures related to implementation of a pilot project are designed to improve the efficiency of WRM in the BNA. Implementation requires actions by federal authorities (at the first stage – development of a legal framework) and regional authorities (implementation of a pilot project).

If the measures prove to be a success, they might be replicated by other regions of the RF provided that relevant decisions are made at the federal level.

Table 3.5. **"Implementability" and estimated period of implementation**

Measure	"Implementability"	Period of implementation	
		Based on the scope of work	Taking into account political, social and economic acceptability
Developing regulatory legal framework and procedural framework for compulsory disclosure of environmental information by enterprises located in the BNA	High	1 year	1 year
Implementing a pilot project in the BNA		1 year	1 year
Organising a campaign to evaluate results of awarding the ratings to enterprises, while making the information available to mass media, and relying on the EID for identifying the most environmentally advanced enterprises		3-6 months	3-6 months

Source: Authors' recommendations and estimates.

The measures appear to be interrelated, and should be implemented in the order above.

Expected outcome

- reduced discharges of hazardous substances into water objects
- public attention to problems relating to the state of ecosystems of Lake Baikal, promoting public involvement in environmental monitoring processes
- a system for interchange of information and data concerning performance indicators to be shared by polluters, and joint measures to this effect.

3.5. Streamlining the system of monitoring of the status of the BNA's ecosystem

Problem description

The responsibility for state environmental monitoring of the ecosystem status of Lake Baikal and the BNA lies with various federal agencies and authorised regional bodies. They consider monitoring and accounting data collected by the relevant federal agencies. Special monitoring of the state of water area of Lake Baikal involves the use of hydro-chemical and hydro-physic-chemical indicators, as well as daily monitoring of the BNA from satellites. Routine measuring of temperature, rise and fall of waves, and water table level in the lake take place at weather stations and testing labs of the Limnological Institute of Siberian Branch of the Russian Academy of Sciences. Information about the state of water and air in the BNA is available in real-time mode on the web sites of the Federal Service of the Russian Federation on Hydrometeorology and Monitoring of the Environment (*Roshydromet*).

According to the authors' estimates, the existing ecosystem monitoring system for Lake Baikal provides essential data for making informed decisions to detect negative trends promptly. At the same time, the system is unable to secure complete, prompt and reliable information about the status of components of the environment within the common information area. In addition, the system does not provide data as required for determining all the parameters ensuing from the present recommendations.

A draft decree of the RF government "On the State of Environmental Monitoring of the Unique Ecological System of Lake Baikal" (the SEM of Baikal) has been designed in response to changes to Federal Law "On Protection of the Environment". The decree comprehensively defines an object of monitoring, and establishes that monitoring of Lake Baikal shall include activities established by Federal Law "On Protection of the Environment". This will include monitoring operational and other activities, types of activities banned or limited in the BNA, requirements to water mode of the lake and requirements to protect flora and fauna (including endemic species) of the BNA. The decree on the SEM of Baikal also assigns responsibilities to federal and local agencies for environmental monitoring of the BNA and for forecasting changes to the ecosystem of Lake Baikal provoked by natural and/or anthropogenic factors.

Federal Target Programme (FTP) "Protection of Lake Baikal and Socio-Economic Development of the Baikal Natural Area" envisages measures to develop the SEM of Baikal and upgrade the state of environmental monitoring network. If fully implemented, the measures shall secure a considerable amount of reliable and timely information. Hence, in respect of the SEM of Baikal, the RF bodies of state power have done thorough preliminary work. *The authors, in general, support the preliminary work, summarise its results and put forward some enhancing proposals within the recommendations*.

Outline of measures

1. Develop regulatory legal framework for state environmental monitoring of the BNA and, to this end, implement the following activities:

- Approve the decree of the RF government "On the State of Environmental Monitoring of the Unique Ecological System of Lake Baikal".
- Amend the decree on State Monitoring of Water objects (RF Government Decree #219 of 10 April 2007) to bring in line with RF Government Decree #681 of 9 August 2013, and extend the list of types of routine monitoring for the status of water objects.

- Develop and approve a sub-programme of state environmental monitoring of the ecosystem of Baikal, as part of the FTP "Protection of Lake Baikal and Socio-Economic Development of the Baikal Natural Area" to increase the status of measures in respect of development of the SEM of Baikal.
- Amend the provision on the Federal Service for Supervision of Natural Resources by discharging the service from regulating the environmental monitoring of the unique ecological system of Lake Baikal.
- Introduce changes into the provision on national natural parks and state-designated wilderness areas of the RF to expand responsibilities for transfer of the results of state environmental monitoring by national natural parks and state-designated wilderness areas to the Ministry of Natural Resources and Environmental Protection of the RF.

2. Expand and re-equip the state network for monitoring for the status of water objects in the RB.

The measure envisages full-scale implementation of the FTP "Protection of Lake Baikal and Socio-Economic Development of the Baikal Natural Area" on the entire territory of the BNA, including Irkutsk Oblast. Efforts shall encompass the introduction of automated monitoring systems; up-to-date monitoring tools, such as biomarkers and supersensitive biosensors; and a system of remote sounding from a satellite. Development of a geo-information portal "Environmental Monitoring of Lake Baikal" will be instrumental.

Estimated incremental cost and fiscal effect

Measure 1 may be implemented as part of the routine work of public authorities. The cost of upgrading the state monitoring network was estimated at RUB 500-800 million (which takes into account the cost of comparable facilities in the RF). Federal funds are the likely source of financing.

Implementing the measures: level of authority and relationship with the Russian Federation's water policy

The recommended measures may be implemented independently. They shall focus mainly on the efficiency of WRM in the BNA. Implementation requires actions by federal authorities.

Table 3.6. **"Implementability" and estimated period of implementation**

Measure	"Implementability"	Period of implementation: Based on the scope of work	Period of implementation: Taking into account political, social and economic acceptability
Developing a regulatory and legal framework for state environmental monitoring of the BNA	High	1 year	1 year
Expanding and re-equipping the state network for monitoring the status of water objects in the RB	Moderate	5-7 years	5-7 years

Source: Authors' recommendations and estimates.

Expected outcome

- improved regulatory and legal framework for state environmental monitoring and monitoring of nature conservation that specifies responsibilities
- more complete, relevant and reliable information about the status of the RB's water objects for reference and assessment purposes
- wider public access to information concerning the SEM of Baikal.

Note

1. Special-purpose state reports "On state of Lake Baikal and measures to protect it" are issued annually.

References

Government of the Russian Federation, Decree "On Approving the State Programme "Protection of the Environment for 2012-2020" (15 April 2014, #326).

Government of the Russian Federation, Decree "On Federal Target Programme "Protection of Lake Baikal and Socio-Economic Development of the Baikal Natural Area in 2012-2020" (21 August 2012, #847).

Government of the Russian Federation, Decree "On the State of Environmental Monitoring of the Unique Ecological System of Lake Baikal" (the SEM of Baikal).

Government of the Russian Federation, Decree #671-p signed 6 May 2008.

SCUCWB for Lake Baikal basin (http://skiovo.enbvu.ru/).

Chapter 4

Improvement of instruments for sustainable use and conservation of water resources in Buryatia

This chapter presents recommendations on improving instruments serving: (a) *to promote sustainable use of water resources (charges for water as a natural resource); and* (b) *limit the pollution of water resources and the environment from both point and diffuse (non-point) sources.*

On top of conventional economic instruments (water abstraction fees and pollution charges) it considers two innovative instruments: (i) *establishing limits for discharges of certain hazardous substances into water objects and a gradual development of markets for quotas for discharges; and* (ii) *introduction of a product tax on substances contributing a lot to diffuse pollution.*

There are two types of pollution of water resources: point source and non-point source (caused by various diffused sources). The relevant technologies to control these two types of pollution vary considerably in international practice (see Report #2). Tax or charges for discharge of polluting substances are imposed to control a limited number of point sources of pollution; the proceeds generally finance water protection measures and cover costs incurred by state structures due to treatment of wastewater and protection of water resources. International practice envisages controlling non-point source pollution caused by diffused sources through such instruments as *(a)* quotas (e.g. for livestock per unit of grazing area in the Netherlands, or for use of nitrogen fertilisers in Denmark); or *(b)* taxes (excise tax) on certain types of products (pesticides, motor oils) that contribute heavily to water pollution; and increased fines for excessive pollution, and so on. Some of the above tools could (and should) be used in the Republic of Buryatia (RB).

4.1. Revision or introduction of water abstraction charge rates

Problem description[1]

In the Russian Federation (RF), payments for water as a resource take the form of a water abstraction fee and a water tax, and are charged by volume. The system of payments for water is used only to replenish the public budget (starting with the federal budget), and does not regulate water consumption. Responsibility for establishing the water abstraction charges structure and rates lies entirely with federal authorities.

The water tax rates and water abstraction fees for Lake Baikal basin appear to be the highest of those applied to all water objects in the RF. The increased rates do not reflect the comparative scarcity of water as a resource in the Republic of Buryatia. In a wider sense, in contrast with best international practices, the charges are not used to regulate the volume and structure of water consumption; at the same time, collected charges for water abstraction are not related to expenditures for water infrastructure maintenance. Moreover, as the fee rates are established by federal rather than regional authorities, the actual rates across the region cannot be conclusively identified (see Report #1).

A draft amendment to the RF Tax Code and draft decree of the RF government[2] envisage increasing water charge rates more than threefold. In this regard, the highest rates remain for Lake Baikal, and rivers and lakes relating to Lake Baikal basin. Increase in water abstraction charges will have a major adverse effect for *Gusinoozerskaya* thermal power plant, which provides electric power for Buryatia; it is a local economic mainstay, as well as a heat supplier to the city of *Gusinoozersk* (population 23 800).

Outline of measures

1. Align the water abstraction fee rates in the RB to averages rates for basins of rivers in the East Siberia region.

Current rates for river basins in Eastern Siberia range from RUB 246-348 per 1 000 cubic metres (m^3) of water withdrawn, while those in respect to rivers and lakes of Lake Baikal basin are set at RUB 576. After the rate increase – with a simultaneous change of category of rates in respect of water objects in Lake Baikal basin – the rates will be at RUB 600-700 per 1 000 m^3 of water withdrawn (with increased fee rates and an unchanged category it would be about RUB 1 483 per 1 000 m^3 according to a draft decree of the RF government).

2. Authorise the regional bodies of state power – in accordance with the RF Code and RF Government Resolution #876 of 30 December 2006 "On rates of charges for the

use of water objects in federal ownership" – to set adjustment multiplying factors for determining the rates of water abstraction fees for the payers (economic agents) who use certain technologies of water abstraction or the water itself. By making use of this right, the regional authorities are supposed to be able to establish "delayed" adjustment multiplying factors in respect of water abstraction charges coming into effect (unless an enterprise changes the old water-intensive technology for a more efficient one by an established date).

The measure has been recommended because a similar instrument is used in international practice (see Report #2). For instance, enterprises operating in water-intensive industries (such as pulp-and-paper plants and tanneries) and using the best available techniques (BAT) and/or relying on water re-use and recycling systems, pay lower water charges; enterprises consuming more water per one tonne of final product, as compared with the average across the industry, pay higher rates of water abstraction fees.

Estimated incremental cost and fiscal effect

Federal budget revenues could be some RUB 250-300 million lower if the rates were increased up to RUB 1 483 per 1 000 m^3 of withdrawn water. However, the fiscal effect cannot be estimated before a decision is made about parameters of change of the taxation system.

Implementing the measures: level of authority and relationship with the Russian Federation's water policy

Implementation of the measures outlined in Table 4.1 requires actions by federal authorities. Measure 1 is oriented towards the enhancement of efficiency of WRM in the BNA. Measure 2 appears to be a common element of the Russian Federation's water policy. The recommended measures may be implemented independently.

Table 4.1. **"Implementability" and estimated period of implementation**

		Period of implementation	
Measure	**"Implementability"**	**Based on the scope of work**	**Taking into account political, social and economic acceptability**
Adjusting the rates of charges for abstraction of water from water objects of the RB to the average rates applied in river basins in Eastern Siberia	Moderate	6 months-1 year	6 months-1 year
Authorising regional state bodies to set multiplying factors for determining water abstraction fee rates for those payers who use certain water abstraction technologies or the water itself.	Low	1 year	2-3 years

Source: Authors' recommendations and estimates.

Expected outcome

- adjusted rates of charges for abstraction of water from water objects of the RB at RUB 600-700 per 1 000 m^3 of water withdrawn – after the increase of rates takes place
- wider use of more water-efficient and environment-friendly ("green") technologies by industrial users, who abstract and withdraw water, and by WSS companies.

4.2. Improving procedures for charging and collection of pollution fees (payments for adverse impact on the environment)

Problem description

Fees for discharging polluting substances into water objects is an economic mechanism for environmental management in the RF, including the BNA. Relevant charges promote economic responsibility for reduction of discharges of polluting substances into water objects. Pollution fees are charged by federal bodies in accordance with standard rates of charges as approved by RF Government Decree #344, 12 December 2003. It allows for discharge of 1 tonne of polluting substances within the maximum allowable emission limit values (MAELVs) and the established temporary limits of discharges. Given the capacity of treatment facilities, it is not feasible to meet the MAELV standards designed for maximum allowable impacts (SMAI) in respect of water objects of Lake Baikal and the rivers associated with its water catchment basin. Authorities and organisations also have problems co-ordinating the introduction of BAT.

An additional multiplying factor, whose value is equal to two, is applied to calculate charges for negative impact on the BNA's environment. The multiplying factor does not take into account different levels of environmental significance of the territories where it is applied (see Report #1). It was assumed that use of the multiplying factor would lead to fewer discharges in the BNA – a territory of special environmental significance. However, the major point-source polluters tend to be utility enterprises that conduct their activity based on regulated tariffs. These rely on state financing for investing in development of treatment facilities. Hence, by setting the rates of charges at the federal level, and encouraging polluters to decrease discharges, no consideration is given to the economic situation of polluters and specificities of the RB are ignored.

There are also some deficiencies in respect to regulating charges for negative impact. First, there are no charges for causing negative impact by changing a water flow regime when using water objects to produce electricity. Second, there is a lack of approved standards for discharges into centralised (piped) sanitation systems.

Outline of measures

1. Establish an Inter-Agency Council for Co-ordination of Activities within the BNA to supervise implementation of BAT and conformity with the MAELVs. This could possibly be within the framework of the Inter-Agency Commission for Conservation of Lake Baikal. The process should engage relevant specialists, including production engineers, hydrologists, hydro-biologists, chemists, etc.

2. Amend regulatory acts to differentiate pollution charge rates according to environmental zones and with due consideration for types of polluting substances; this would replace uniform multiplying factor "2" in respect of the entire BNA.

The above amendments concerns the RF Government Decree #344, 12 June 2003 and the guidelines for designing standards for allowable discharges of substances and microorganisms into water objects by water users approved by the *Minprirody* of the Russian Federation (Order #333, 17 December 2007). With regard to the BNA, it is recommended to introduce additional multiplying factors in respect to basic rates of charges for polluting effluents differentiated according to environmental zones and with due account for environmental capacity of territories evaluated in the course of research.

3. Add a change in water flow regime (when water objects are used to produce electricity) to the types of allowable impact on water objects and respectively amend the guidelines for designing standards for maximum allowable impact on water objects approved by the *Minprirody* of the Russian Federation (Order #328, 12 December 2007).

4. Revise the standards of the maximum allowable discharges into centralised sanitation systems and their users with due consideration of the feasibility of reaching the above limits within the BNA.

Estimated incremental cost and fiscal effect

Measures 1 and 3 presented in Table 4.2 may be carried out as part of the routine activities by the *Minprirody* of the Russian Federation. Direct incremental costs and direct influence on budget revenue appear to be non-existent in respect of the above measures. Estimated cost of the research into differentiation of charges according to environmental zones and with due account for environmental capacity of territories (Measure 2) may be up to RUB 50 million. Estimated cost of the research relating to Measure 4 may be RUB 20-30 million.

Implementing the measures: level of authority and relationship with the Russian Federation's water policy

The recommended measures may be carried out independently. Implementation of Measure 1 requires action by regional authorities of the RB. It is recommended to set up an Inter-Agency Council for Co ordination of Activities within the BNA to supervise implementation of the BAT and ensure conformity with the MAELVs. Implementation of Measures 2-4 requires actions by federal authorities. Measure 3 is a common element of the Russian Federation's water policy, while Measure 2 and Measure 4 are designed to improve the efficiency of WRM in the BNA.

Table 4.2. **"Implementability" and estimated period of implementation**

Measure	"Implementability"	Period of implementation	
		Based on the scope of work	Taking into account political, social and economic acceptability
Establishing the Inter-Agency Council for Co-ordination of Activities within the BNA to supervise implementation of the BAT and conformity with the MAELVs	High	1 year	1 year
Amending regulatory acts to differentiate pollution charge rates according to environmental zones and with due consideration for types of polluting substances and microorganisms	Low	5-6 years	5-6 years
Adding in a change in water flow regime, when using water objects for production of electricity, to the types of allowable impact on water objects	Moderate	3-5 years	3-5 years
Revising standards for maximum allowable discharges into centralised (piped) sanitation systems and their users with due consideration of the feasibility of reaching the said limits within the BNA.	Low	3-5 years	5-7 years

Source: Authors' recommendations and estimates.

Expected outcome

- new MAELVs informed by the BAT and technical capacity of the relevant facilities
- adopted operational guidelines on use of the BAT, including in respect of treatment facilities, by major polluters in the BNA
- enhanced procedures for charging for negative impact on the environment to reduce the volume of polluting effluents in the Central Environmental Zone (CEZ) via gradual introduction of the BAT and conformity with MAELVs.

4.3. Establishing limits for discharges of certain hazardous substances into water objects and a gradual development of markets for quotas for discharges

Problem description

As is evident from previous stages of work, the RB is lacking enabling mechanisms to encourage polluters to reduce discharges into water objects and implement relevant environmental actions. A solution might be firstly to establish aggregate daily limit of discharges of certain polluting substances into water objects. Having in mind that in the long run, enterprises that systematically meet the established limits will be allowed to transfer to third parties the right for the underused quotas for discharging specific pollutants (including on fee-based agreements) (see Report #1).

The proposed measure relies on relevant international experience. Trade in pollution quotas requires the creation of a market of **tradable pollution rights (quotas)**. The market provides for decline in pollution thanks to the enterprises with the lowest marginal pollution abatement cost (costs associated with reduction of an extra unit of discharges). Trade in permits for discharges is a universal and flexible instrument that is more “loyal” to polluters than administrative bans, or penalty rates for discharges above the allowed limit. The use of pollution quotas eventually ensures the possibility of reducing the level of environmental pollution at minimal costs for society compared with charges and penalties for discharges used in the RF.

Markets of trade in permits (quotas) for discharges are regulated by ad hoc legislation establishing ownership rights to these permits, mechanism of trade and defining concrete structures responsible for the management and monitoring of discharges and of trade in permits (see Report #2).

The use of trade in quotas is virtually non-existent in regulation of environmental management and protection of natural resources in the RF. The arrival of the new market, hence, shall entail serious administrative efforts. In addition, prior to its practical verification, the system may cause concern given the significance of the ecosystem in the BNA. For this reason, the first (pilot) stage mechanism should be used in a limited manner; this implies that enterprises regularly falling within discharge limits can transfer (sell) their right for underused effluent volumes of certain substances to a third party. At the initial stage, the instrument may be used only with regard to individual types of pollutants (e.g. biochemical oxygen demand (BOD) and chemical oxygen demand (COD), total and ammonia nitrogen, phosphorus, fats and oil products, heavy metals, etc.) and individual water objects.

Outline of measures

1. Amend federal environmental laws by setting limits (including daily limits) on volume of discharges of certain chemical substances (e.g. BOD, COD, nitrogen, phosphorus, etc.) into water objects.

2. Amend federal laws to enable introduction of trade in permits (quotas) for discharges of the above specific polluting substances, and the implementation of a pilot project in the RB.

It is recommended that the above-mentioned provisions be established in respect of the BNA as a pilot region. A body of state power of the RB (for instance, the Ministry of Natural Resources) should be authorised to issue the permits (quotas).

3. Implement, in the RB, a pilot project to establish limits for discharges of pollutants and progressive development of the market of pollution quotas. The stages of implementation are as follows:

- Develop and approve guidelines for determining the maximum allowable aggregate daily discharge of key polluting substances in respect of all the economic entities on the selected water courses (at the first stage, the River Selenga basin could be selected).
- Provide administrative and technical support in regard to the system of monitoring and accounting of discharges and trading in permits in compliance with regulating federal documents.
- Implement the system of monitoring and the market of quotas for discharges.

An important aspect here relates to the necessity of a sound combination and interaction of two economic instruments – establishing quotas for discharges and related trading schema, and pollution charges (payment for negative environmental impact) in order to avoid double taxation. In every single case, an enterprise, as an economic agent, will choose what is more appropriate and beneficial for it – to pay penalty rates for excess discharges or to buy the respective quota (equal to excess discharge of specific pollutants) not used by other economic agents. International experience shows that a sound combination of these two economic instruments might generate significant positive results.

No less important for the efficiency and effectiveness of the above instruments is the need for the introduction of an adequate emission (discharges) **monitoring and accounting system** and a system of **enforcement and compliance**. These systems should be strict enough to not allow enterprises (polluters) to bypass the regulation and violate their obligations.

Estimated incremental cost and fiscal effect

The cost of preparatory work was estimated at RUB 20-30 million. The funding is needed to develop guidelines for determining the maximum allowable aggregate daily discharge and to provide administrative support. The proposed amount reflects the need for research into the impact of various activities on the state of biosphere in the BNA in order to assess maximum allowable impact. Conversely, the above-indicated amount does not take into account the cost of technical support in respect to the system of monitoring and pollution inventory, or the cost of capacity development in public authorities responsible for pollution monitoring and inventory, and for establishing and regulating the market for quotas. The relevant cost estimate needs special research.

The RF budget is likely to be the source of funds. Direct influence on budget revenue appears to be non-existent in regard to the measures.

Table 4.3. **"Implementability" and estimated period of implementation**

Measure	"Implementability"	Period of implementation	
		Based on the scope of work	Taking into account political, social and economic acceptability
Amending federal environmental laws by establishing daily limits for discharges of certain polluting substances into water objects	Moderate	6 months-1 year	6 months-1 year
Amending federal laws to introduce trade in permits (quotas) for discharges of certain polluting substances into water objects, and implementation of a pilot project in the RB	Low	6 months-1 year	6 months-1 year
Implementing, in the RB, a pilot project to establish limits for discharges of pollutants and develop the market for quotas for discharges.		2-3 years	2-3 years

Source: Authors' recommendations and estimates.

Implementing the measures: level of authority and relationship with the Russian Federation's water policy

The measure might seek to attain the efficiency of WRM in the BNA, or in the RF overall, depending on scale of implementation. The measures outlined in Table 4.4 require joint actions by federal and regional authorities. The foregoing measures appear to be interrelated and, hence, should be implemented in the order recommended above.

Expected outcome

- established daily limits for discharges of certain polluting substances into water-specific objects in the BNA
- pilot implementation of a system of permits and creation of a market for quotas for discharges in the RB, with subsequent dissemination of the relevant practice in other regions of the Russian Federation.

4.4. Introduction of a charge (tax) on toxic agricultural chemicals (pesticides, herbicides, etc.) and on synthetic detergents

Problem description

The use of pesticides, herbicides and other agro-chemicals is a prerequisite for obtaining sustainable yields of agricultural crops. Yet regular use of persistent high-toxic pesticides, especially in excessive amounts, has a detrimental effect on ecosystems and the health of humans and animals. Synthetic detergents also have a negative effect on water resources because they comprise surface acting agents along with phosphorus agents. In regard to the BNA, this appears to be of particular importance in view of the need to protect the ecosystem of Lake Baikal.

In the Russian Federation, the use of pesticides relies on "State catalogue of pesticides and agrichemicals approved for use in the territory of the Russian Federation", which provides the list of permitted pesticides and herbicides. In general, RF regulations are less stringent than the relevant recommendation of the World Health Organization (WHO).

In the BNA, special constraints on the use of toxic agrichemicals are established and applied only in the CEZ. In respect of synthetic detergents, constraints are non-existent. Expert panels during the project singled out that it would be expedient to strengthen the use of the above-mentioned substances within the BNA. According to the RB's ecologists, **phosphorus synthetic detergents kill sponge that can filter and, thus, purify water in Lake Baikal**. At the same time, the negative impact of agrichemicals and synthetic detergents on water quality still requires further research.

As is evident from international practice, the introduction of charges (e.g. excise tax) on use of toxic pesticides, herbicides and other agrichemicals, and on synthetic detergents may serve to regulate use efficiently (see Report #2). Considering that the foregoing charges (taxes) are inapplicable in the RF, Buryatia may become a pilot site for elaborating the recommended practice.

Outline of measures

1. Evaluate the impact of agrichemicals and synthetic detergents on the ecosystem of the BNA, assessing the feasibility of prohibiting the use of most toxic ones and reducing the intensity of use of the foregoing substances based on the introduction of charges (taxes).

The first stage involves preparation of a list of agrichemicals (pesticides, herbicides, etc.) that tend to be the most toxic and hazardous to the environment, biodiversity and human health. The WHO's classifier could help develop the list.

In addition, research is needed into the impact of agrichemicals and synthetic detergents on Lake Baikal and into the anthropogenic impact on the BNA (see sub-section 2.3.3). The impact on agriculture should also be taken into account when assessing the feasibility of prohibiting the use, or reducing the intensity of use, of toxic agrochemicals.

Building on the research, two lists will be prepared. One will list substances totally prohibited in the BNA, while the other will list substances whose use is subject to a special charge (tax); the amount of the relevant rates of charges (taxes) will accompany these lists. The rates of charges (taxes) should be differentiated by toxicity level and by effect of substances on the environment, ecosystem and human health.

2. Prohibit use of the most toxic agrichemicals and introduce charges (taxes) on the use of permitted agrichemicals and synthetic detergents through the following actions:

- Include legal provisions on prohibiting use of the above-mentioned most hazardous substances and on introduction of charges (taxes) for use of permitted agrichemicals and synthetic detergents into federal legislation (Federal Law "On Protection of Lake Baikal", the RF Tax Code and other laws).
- Provide legal advice and administrative support to introduce charges (taxes) and supervise compliance with bans at the regional level.

Special attention should be paid to *selecting a mechanism and scale for introduction of the recommended charges (taxes)*. In this regard, the following options shall be envisaged:

- Levy charges (taxes) on the sale or use of the products in question.
- Introduce charges (taxes) within the BNA (in the RB, or simultaneously in the RB and Irkutsk Oblast) or within the entire territory of the RF.

In regard to synthetic detergents, charges (taxes) might be levied on the sale of products irrespective of scale of use. In the event that the relevant mechanism is applied exclusively within the BNA, a special regional charge (tax) should be levied. The use of the mechanism at the federal level would require an excise tax (and the equivalent import duty).

As for the use of pesticides, herbicides and other agrichemicals, the all-national introduction of the mechanism might entail both the levying of charges (taxes) on the production and import into the RF and on the sale of products in question within the RF (in the form of an excise tax and an equivalent export duty). Organising the pilot project only within the BNA is deemed to be complex. On the one hand, the levying of tax on the sale (sales tax) would make tax administration easier. On the other, such a tax introduced solely in the RB could encourage large-scale tax dodging (by purchasing taxed chemicals outside the BNA and using them in the BNA). At the same time, the levying of the taxes on legal entities that use agrochemicals in the RB would be even more complex, and levying it on individuals would be almost impossible to administer.

Estimated incremental cost and fiscal effect

The measures may be part of the routine activities of public authorities. The introduction of charges (taxes) on agrichemicals with rates differentiated according to toxicity level of the taxable products might have an effect on agriculture in the region where it's applied. The relevant estimates and assessments of potential fiscal revenues from the levy require analysis beyond the scope of the project.

Implementing the measures: level of authority and relationship with the Russian Federation's water policy

The measure might seek to attain the efficiency of WRM in the BNA, or in the RF overall, depending on scale of implementation. The measures outlined in Table 4.4 shall be implemented jointly by federal and regional authorities.

Table 4.4. **"Implementability" and estimated period of implementation**

Measure	"Implementability"	Period of implementation	
		Based on the scope of work	Taking into account political, social and economic acceptability
Evaluating the impact of agrichemicals and synthetic detergents on the ecosystem of the BNA, assessing the feasibility of prohibiting the use of most toxic agrochemicals or reducing the intensity of use of the substances in question.	Low	6 months-1 year	6 months-1 year
Prohibiting the use of the most toxic agrichemicals and introducing charges (taxes) on the use of permitted agrichemicals and on synthetic detergents		1-2 years	3-4 years

Source: Authors' recommendations and estimates.

The foregoing measures appear to be interrelated and, hence, should be implemented in the order recommended above.

Expected outcome

- more efficient (and reduced) use and circulation of pesticides and herbicides and of synthetic detergents in the RB and/or across the RF
- reduced non-point source (diffuse) pollution of water resources in the RB (or in the RF in general) from toxic agrichemicals, surface acting agents and phosphorus agents.

4.5. Upgrading a system of waste management in the BNA, and promoting safe management of environmentally damaging products and waste

Problem description

A dire problem facing the ecosystem of the RB and in terms of negative impact on water resources consists of improper management of solid and liquid municipal wastes, including domestic wastes. The following factors underlie the problem:

- The system of collection, transportation and disposal of waste from the CEZ of the BNA used in the RB appears to be unable to fully protect the water objects from non-point source (diffuse) pollution, while coastal areas and surface water objects are polluted by garbage.
- Lack of economic incentives and administrative enforcement measures for compliance with laws and regulations leads to pollution of water resources (leachate from dump sites, illegal placement of garbage, littering of coastal areas).
- The RB lacks a sound system of managing domestic and industrial wastes, including their re-use and recycling. This results in designating considerable land plots in the RB for placement of solid wastes.
- Capacity of existing infrastructure for collection and treatment of waste motor oils, bilge water from vessels does not match the scale of navigation.
- As is evident, the practice of levying penalties for violation of water and environmental laws suffers from inadequate administrative enforcement.
- Local governments authorised to handle waste management issues fail to fulfil their functions because of inadequate financing.

The problem is urgent. Tourism promotion by regional power bodies in the RB will bring more anthropogenic load on the region, in particular on the BNA. This implies an increase in both water abstraction and wastewater discharges into water objects. Pollution with solid and liquid domestic wastes contribute to the deterioration of the environmental situation in the BNA.

Improper management of environmentally damaging consumption waste is another pressing problem in the RB. There is no system of separate waste collection of used mercury and fluorescent containing tubes, accumulators, batteries, electrical equipment and office machines, and large household appliances (refrigerators, air-conditioners, etc.) in the region. As a result, environmentally damaging waste gets mixed with household waste, allowing hazardous substances to enter the environment and water objects.

Outline of measures

In the opinion of the authors, measures to promote sustainable environmental development of the RB should also envisage a safe system of waste management, reuse and recycling of waste. The system should address the following tasks:

- Minimise waste generation.
- Recycle or reuse waste[3] (in line with the OECD **3Rs** concept: *reduce, re-use, recycle*).
- Locate facilities engaged in management of consumption waste containing hazardous substances outside the CEZ and outside the BNA, where feasible.
- Promote safe treatment, recycling, placement and disposal of waste, especially environmentally damaging waste, which can cause environmental damage.
- Optimise logistics, transportation and processing of waste.
- Rehabilitate land polluted with waste.

With a view to implementing the identified tasks, the following actions are recommended:

1. Assign responsibility for waste management to regional authorities. This implies amending the federal laws on waste management and on responsibilities of public authorities, and adopting the relevant bylaws.

2. Develop a legal framework in respect of waste management and location of facilities for managing the waste containing hazardous substances in the RB. This involves the implementation of the following measures:

- Approve a legal framework for creation of a waste management system and locating facilities for managing hazardous waste in the RB.
- Approve a concept and regional scheme of waste management and location of facilities for managing hazardous waste outside CEZ or the BNA, where reasonable, and provide for reasonable transport from collection areas to places of treatment and disposal.

3. Establish a regional operator responsible for waste management. This operator should organise the following in the territory of the RB: collection, transportation and disposal of solid and liquid domestic wastes of all hazard categories, including hazardous waste; separation of waste that can be recycled or reused; clean-up and re-cultivation of functioning dump sites and waste accumulation sites in the territory of the BNA.

4. Implement measures oriented towards cleaning the RB, starting with the CEZ, closing and re-cultivating waste disposal sites that fail to meet environmental requirements.

5. Create legal and economic prerequisites for wastewater re-use and recycling, particularly by allocating land plots for construction of waste management (recycling) facilities, promoting the participation of the RB in organisations engaged in waste management and extending state guarantees on loans. In regard to managing the recycling process, special emphasis should be placed on close co-operation of the state and business community to improve the environmental situation without detriment to economic development.

6. Tighten control and responsibility for observance of sanitary and environmental requirements in the BNA, increase the amount of penalties for violation (introducing the relevant amendments into the RF Administrative Offences Code) and increase the number of staff.

Estimated incremental cost and fiscal effect

The cost of Measures 4 and 5 is estimated at RUB 1.1 million (based on the cost of comparable facilities in the RF). The funds from private investors shall go mainly to finance construction of facilities for treatment of environmentally damaging waste; state funds shall be spent to create landfills, closing and re-cultivating waste disposal sites (dump sites) that fail to meet the environmental requirements and cleaning areas polluted with garbage. State financing of the measures should be distributed between authorities and an ad hoc (dedicated) fund for support to the BNA provided such a fund is established (see sub-section 2.5.2).

Measures 1 and 2 could be implemented as part of the routine work of public authorities. Cost estimates for Measure 3 (creation of a regional operator) and Measure 6 (as it relates to increasing staff) require special research.

Implementing the measures: level of authority and relationship with the Russian Federation's water policy

Implementation of Measures 1 and 6 requires actions by federal authorities. Regional authorities have power to implement Measures 2-5 (see Table 4.5).

Measure 1 concerns the entire territory of the RF. Other measures focus on enhancing the efficiency of WRM and management of the ecosystem of Lake Baikal, in general.

Measures 1-3 are interrelated, and should be implemented in the order presented. Measures 4-6 could be carried out independently.

Table 4.5. **"Implementability" and estimated period of implementation**

		Period of implementation	
Measure	**"Implementability"**	**Based on the scope of work**	**Taking into account political, social and economic**
Assigning responsibility for waste management to regional authorities	High	6 months	6 months
Further developing a legal framework in respect of waste management and location of facilities for treatment of hazardous waste in the RB	High	1 year	1 year
Establishing a regional operator for waste management for the entire RB	High	6 months	6 months
Cleaning dump sites the RB, starting with the CEZ, closing and re-cultivating the sites of waste disposal that presently fail to meet environmental requirements	Low	1-2 years	5-6 years
Creating legal and economic prerequisites for waste reuse and recycling	Low	1-2 years	3-4 years
Tightening control and responsibility for the monitoring of sanitary and environmental requirements in the BNA	Moderate	1-2 years	1-2 years

Source: Authors' recommendations and estimates.

Expected outcome

In the short term:

- a unified operator is established responsible for waste management in the BNA, including collection, transportation, safe treatment and disposal
- reduced level of pollution with garbage in the BNA, and clean-up of dump sites
- a system of safe management of waste of consumption that ensures minimal impact on the environment in the RB.

In the medium term:

- closed and re-cultivated dump sites and other waste disposal sites that presently fail to meet the environmental requirements
- a system of separate collection and treatment of waste, including the waste of high hazard category and valuable components of household waste (recyclables)
- broader reuse of individual types of hazardous waste
- a sustainable scheme of incentives to encourage compliance with sanitary and environmental requirements in the BNA.

Notes

1. For more detail, see Sections 1.4. and 3.0 of Report #1 prepared under the project, and the 2013 Report.
2. See the new governmental decree # 1509 of 26 December 2014 "On rates of charges for the use of water objects in federal ownership, and amendments of Section 1 on rates of charges for the use of water objects in federal ownership".
3. Re-used glass and plastic bottles (containers), regenerated waste motor oils or their use for heating of social and commercial facilities; and the use of recoverable materials produced as a result of recycling valuable components of production and consumption waste – glass, plastic, metal, paper and cardboard, etc.

References

Government of the Russian Federation, Decree #344, 12 June 2003.

Government of the Russian Federation, Decree #344, 12 June 2003.

Government of the Russian Federation, Decree "On Federal Target Programme "Protection of Lake Baikal and Socio-Economic Development of the Baikal Natural Area in 2012-2020" (21 August 2012, #847).

Chapter 5

Instruments for ensuring higher capitalisation of the Baikal Natural Area

This chapter presents recommendations on how to apply economic instruments for conservation of the ecosystem in, and to increase capitalisation of, the Baikal Natural Area (BNA) when conducting economic activities within its territory. The following is recommended:

– lifting or softening administrative bans on some activities along with a wider use of economic instruments for managing economic activities in the central environmental zone of the BNA;

– introduction of payment for ecosystem services;

– providing state support to environment-oriented activities to improve capitalisation of the BNA; and

– redistribution of hydro-energy rent captured by the cascade of hyrdo-electric stations on Angara river downstream and introduction of a mechanism of compensation for environmental damage caused to the Baikal ecosystem and to the economy of coastal districts by operations of the stations.

In this report, *capitalisation* of BNA is understood as transformation of natural resources (including water and biodiversity), ecosystem services and aesthetic value of nature and landscapes located in the BNA into economic assets able to generate revenues and other economic benefits, and assigning monetary value to the assets, economic activities and businesses operating on the BNA territory. It could be assigned by market (if it exists) or through a dedicated monetary evaluation by qualified experts.

Valuation of the economic and monetary value of natural capital is an important prerequisite for sustainable use of natural resources and their sound regulation and management. In this regard, the task consists of identification of adequate qualitative measures for valuation of natural resources (natural capital) similar to other components of national wealth. This gives an opportunity for adequate identification of a pool of non-financial assets in the system of national accounts (SNA). In this regard, integration of natural resources in the pool of economic assets of the country means that these resources are considered as natural capital.

To ensure sustainable natural resource use, it is necessary to include ecosystem services and natural resources in the economic accounting system.

Sometimes implementation of such economic valuation and assessment is rather complicated. Nevertheless, for the Republic of Buryatia, adequate valuation of natural capital of the BNA provides for assessing its actual economic importance. Identifying actual economic and monetary value of natural resources, and ways to enhance it, provides for increasing capitalisation of the area where those assets are located. It also provides stimulus for its further economic development.

Until recently, adequate valuation of natural capital and assessment of the economic and monetary value of natural resources were a problem and task both for the country in general and for its specific regions (provinces). In this regard, the BNA is not an exclusion at all. The system of bans and limitations for economic activities in the BNA inevitably has an impact on the economic and monetary value of its natural capital. Partial waiver of limitations on economic activity and on development of environmentally-friendly businesses in the BNA will provide for increasing capitalisation of BNA itself and higher economic and monetary value of its natural capital.

Only part of the potential economic value of natural resources is reflected in present market prices, while the other part cannot be easily identified in market processes. As a result, their actual value is not adequately reflected (or even not taken into account) in economic development decisions. This, in turn, eventually causes costly mistakes in economic policy and strategic planning related to deficit of natural assets, neglecting the traditional notion of local population of value of certain resources and expediency of specific types of natural resource use.

Moreover, in the assessment of costs of projects and decision making, existing economic analysis does not take into account so-called externalities. In this regard, payment for ecosystem services (PES) and taking adequate measures for their development play more important roles. It helps to make adequate valuation of the economic and monetary value of natural capital and significantly increase its value. Underestimation of the role and the economic value of ecosystem services lead to inadequate management decisions in the field of natural resource use. In the end, this causes significant economic losses and sometimes even damages the environment and natural resources.

The above considerations determine the structure and logic of this chapter devoted to characteristic of economic instruments aimed at the development and increasing capitalisation of the Baikal natural area.

5.1. Evaluation of natural capital of the Baikal ecosystem

Problem description

The location of Lake Baikal within the boundaries of the RB creates a competitive advantage for the region's development. At present, however, the region enjoys few economic gains from Lake Baikal. It underestimates and underuses the lake's location as a development resource.

In the opinion of the authors and of a vast majority of specialists who have taken part in elaborating the present recommendations, and considering the constraints on economic activity in the CEZ of the BNA, *sustainable and a more autonomous development of the RB shall be possible only due to, and through a higher capitalisation of, the natural capital of Lake Baikal*.

Capitalisation of the natural capital of the BNA via use and promotion of ecosystem services and supporting environment-oriented activities, among others, is a prerequisite for sustainable development of the RB. It is also needed for securing adequate *financial inflow* (income), and financing projects that support and develop the water sector. Current financing has been insufficient to develop the region. In this regard, the monetary evaluation of the natural capital of Lake Baikal has been proposed as a special recommendation.

Outline of measures

1. Implement activities to assess and evaluate in economic and monetary terms the natural capital of the ecosystem of Lake Baikal.

Relevant work should be carried out within the framework of FTP "Protection of Lake Baikal and Socio-Economic Development of the Baikal Natural Area". The first stage involves the development of a methodology for economic and monetary evaluation of natural capital with due consideration of international practice, specificities of the BNA and management of natural resources in the RF in general.

International experience (e.g. United Kingdom) suggests that several steps are needed before engaging in a costly fully-fledged evaluation exercise. First, it would make sense to **rank** (in qualitative terms) different components of the natural capital and various ecosystem services. Second, a detailed economic and monetary evaluation should be made starting from the most valuable components and services.

Next steps should include the work as described below:

- Assess potential economic and fiscal benefits of introduction of payment for ecosystem services and develop the instrument in the BNA (with due consideration of results of respective research and field study).
- Justify the choice of priorities in regard to developing environment-oriented activities and relevant support measures.
- Prepare draft laws to regulate the introduction of payment for ecosystem services.
- Estimate potential gains in terms of accelerated development of the BNA.

2. Develop a concept of promotion of environment-oriented activities and introduction of payments for ecosystem services with a view to protecting and restoring water catchment and the ecosystem in the BNA.

Estimated incremental cost and fiscal effect

The cost of proposed measures may be estimated at up to RUB 25 million for the first stage (methodology), and at RUB 200-300 million for the second stage (comprehensive research). Expert estimates are based on the cost of a major research on environmental subjects in the RF.

Implementing the measures: level of authority and relationship with the Russian Federation's water policy

Measures outlined in Table 5.1 aim to enhance the efficiency of WRM in the BNA. Implementation thereof requires actions by federal authorities. The interrelated measures shall be implemented in the order as recommended above.

Table 5.1. **"Implementability" and estimated period of implementation**

Measure	"Implementability"	Period of implementation	
		Based on the scope of work	Taking into account political, social and economic acceptability
Evaluating the natural capital of the ecosystem of Lake Baikal	Moderate	2-3 years	2-3 years
Developing a concept of using and promoting environment-oriented activities and introducing PES with a view to protecting and restoring water-catchment and water-protection functions of the ecosystem in the BNA		2-3 years	2-3 years

Source: Authors' recommendations and estimates.

Expected outcome

- a methodological framework for the economic and monetary evaluation of the natural capital and the ecosystem in the BNA
- priority measures to facilitate, as much as possible, the accelerated socio-economic development of the BNA through payments for ecosystem services and promotion of environment-oriented activities in the BNA, among other ways.

5.2. Harmonisation of system of environmental regulation in the BNA

Problem description

The RF legislation establishes a system of strict environmental regulation of economic activities in the BNA. The system, however, has gaps because some regulatory acts on economic activities and environmental protection in the BNA are missing. Though envisaged by the federal law "On Protection of Lake Baikal", the regulatory sub-law acts have not yet been adopted.

Moreover, some technical deficiencies in environmental regulation of economic activities in the BNA must be repaired. In the first place, this implies revising the SMAI, as it applies to Lake Baikal (including limits for discharges of polluting substances) and justifying the environmental standards. Standards should be advised and procedures adjusted, taking into account findings of research to determine the effects of anthropogenic impact on the state of the ecosystem of Lake Baikal (see sub-section 2.3.3).

Outline of measures

1. Develop and approve regulatory (sub-law) legal acts envisaged in the federal law "On Protection of Lake Baikal", which implies the following:

- Determine and approve, by a relevant decree of the RF government, the boundaries of the water conservation area (WCA) of Lake Baikal, preparing a list of facilities in the WCA.
- Develop and approve, by a relevant decree of the RF government, the Regulations for Clean-up or Conversion of Environmentally Damaging Facilities within the CEZ of the BNA.
- Develop and approve, by a relevant decree of the RF government, the Regulations for Organisation of Tourism and Recreation in the CEZ of the BNA in conformity with the regulations enforcing the observance of the maximum allowable environmental load.

2. Provide a deeper justification and substantiation of environmental standards as they apply to performance of economic activities in the BNA, taking into account research into the effects of anthropogenic impact on the state of the ecosystem of Lake Baikal:

- Revise the SMAI as it applies to the ecosystem of Lake Baikal.
- Elaborate environmental standards, and assess and forecast their environmental, social, and economic impact.

Estimated incremental cost and fiscal effect

The measures presented in Table 5.2 may be carried out as part of the routine activities of public authorities with no direct incremental costs. Direct influence on budget revenue appears to be non-existent (expenses for the above research were considered in sub-section 2.3.3.).

Implementing the measures: level of authority and relationship with the Russian Federation's water policy

Implementation of Measure 1 aimed to enhance efficiency of WRM in the BNA requires actions by federal authorities. While regional authorities of the RB have sufficient power to implement measures as they relate to approving the Regulations for Organisation of Tourism and Recreation in the CEZ of the BNA and organising for the recommended research.

Table 5.2. **"Implementability" and estimated period of implementation**

Measure	"Implementability"	Period of implementation	
		Based on the scope of work	Taking into account political, social and economic acceptability
Developing and approving regulatory legal acts provided for in Federal Law "On Protection of Lake Baikal"	Moderate	1-3 years	3-5 years
Providing a deeper justification of environmental standards as they apply to performance of economic activities in the BNA, taking into account research into the anthropogenic impact on the state of the ecosystem of Lake Baikal	Moderate	1-2 years	3-4 years

Source: Authors' recommendations and estimates.

The recommended measures may be carried out independently.

Expected outcome

- harmonised relevant laws and sub-laws and improved environmental regulation of economic activities in the BNA
- promotion of economic activities in the RB along with preservation of the integrity of the ecosystem of Lake Baikal.

5.3. Lifting or softening some administrative bans along with a wider use of economic instruments for managing economic activities in the central environmental zone of the BNA

Problem description

Restrictions applied in the BNA and environmental requirements increase production costs and entail lost economic opportunities for the republic (due to the bans and restrictions, the Republic of Buryatia loses 5-7% of gross regional product (GRP) annually, according to regional authorities). This means that environmental bans and restrictions reduce the standard of living in the region.

A case study in the RB within the project gives grounds to recommend lifting or softening some of the administrative instruments applied to the BNA, replacing them with a wider use of economic instruments. In keeping with international practice, if potential environmental damage turns out to be unacceptable, administrative instruments such as bans, or strict performance standards, should be applied. If potential damage appears to be minor or non-critical (e.g. if even excessive discharge of a pollutant does not cause any critical damage to the ecosystem), the focus would be typically on creating incentives by means of economic (and other) instruments (see Reports #1 and#2). **This approach is also recommended for the BNA.**

In 2014, several bans previously imposed on certain economic activities in the CEZ of the BNA were lifted, including the following:

- a ban on construction of buildings and facilities of the enterprises, if the latter conducts business in a manner not damaging to the environment
- a ban on bottling of drinking water and on processing of vegetables and berries from household gardens and farming enterprises, production of herbal medicines, etc.

By the authors' estimates, lifting the bans would improve the prospects of socio-economic development in the RB without causing considerable increase of environmental risks.

However, justification of a possible lifting or softening of the existing administrative bans requires more research. The limits of acceptable mitigation of bans and constraints, in the context of their impact on the ecosystem of the CEZ, have not yet been established. Although relevant research does take place, it generally focuses on other aspects than how to mitigate the bans, while taking into account actual or potential damage to the ecosystem.

At the same time as the RB lifted bans, federal laws made environmental impact assessment mandatory in respect of construction and rehabilitation of any real estate located in the BNA. This considerably increases both the period for securing a construction permit and ensuing costs.

Outline of measures

1. Research into the impact of various types of economic activities on the state of biosphere of the BNA.

Some research should be conducted to detect the impact of various types of activity (and, in some cases, the impact of certain facilities and entities) on the biosphere of the BNA. Relevant works should be carried out within the framework of FTP "Protection of Lake Baikal and Socio-Economic Development of the Baikal Natural Area". The impact of permafrost on the level of pollution of groundwater in the RB, detected at the first stage of the project, requires special research.

2. Amend the RF Government Decree "On Approving the List of the Types of Activities Prohibited in the Central Environmental Zone of the Baikal National Area" (#643, 31 August 2001), as it relates to revision of the list of prohibited types of activities, with due account for research findings.

The complete ban on a range of activities necessary for normal functioning and development of settlements in the central environmental zone should be revised in line with the above-mentioned principles. The list of acceptable changes shall be based on research to determine the allowable volumes and zones of deforestation and forest harvesting, construction of transport, energy infrastructure, utilities, etc.

3. Amend Federal Law "On Environmental Impact Assessment" (#174-ФЗ, 23 November 1995) as it relates to specifying the list of objects of state environmental impact assessment to be carried out at the federal level.

The above federal assessment should be carried out only in respect of the facilities that might have considerable impact on the ecosystem of Lake Baikal.

Estimated incremental cost and fiscal effect

The cost of the recommended research may be estimated at RUB 300-500 million (expert estimates are based on the cost of a major research on environmental subjects in the RF).

The potential positive economic effects from lifting or softening existing administrative bans are estimated at 1-1.5% of GRP, and up to RUB 200-300 million of extra tax proceeds, annually, to the RF budget.

Implementing the measures: level of authority and relationship with the Russian Federation's water policy

Implementation of the measures outlined in Table 5.3 requires actions by federal authorities, which focus on enhancing the efficiency of WRM in the BNA.

Table 5.3. **"Implementability" and estimated period of implementation**

Measure	"Implementability"	Period of implementation	
		Based on the scope of work	Taking into account political, social and economic acceptability
Researching into the impact of various types of activities on the state of biosphere of the BNA	Low	2-3 years	2-3 years
Amending the RF Government Decree "On Approving the List of the Types of Activities Prohibited in the Central Environmental Zone of the Baikal National Area" (#643, 31 August 2001), as it relates to revising the list of prohibited types of activities, with due consideration for research findings		2-3 years	3-4 years
Amending Federal Law "On Environmental Impact Assessment" (#174-Ф3, 23 November 1995) as it relates to specifying the list of objects of state environmental impact assessment to be carried out at the federal level	Moderate	6 months-1 year	1-2 years

Source: Authors' recommendations and estimates.

Measures 1 and 2 appear to be interrelated, and should be implemented in the order presented. Measure 3 could be carried out independently.

Expected outcome

- a defined maximum allowable burden on environment and volumes of abstraction of natural resources (including in respect of certain types of activities)
- lower administrative barriers to construction and rehabilitation of facilities in the BNA
- a more enabling environment for normal performance and development of settlements in the CEZ, and accelerated socio-economic development in the BNA through payment for ecosystem services and promotion of environment-oriented activities in the BNA.

5.4. State support to environment-oriented activities to improve capitalisation of the BNA

Problem description

State support to environment-oriented activities in the RB consists mainly of financing the development of tourism infrastructure and industry under respective FTPs and RTPs. Public financing (from the republican budget) also supports waste management system in Buryatia. In the authors' opinion, the support appears to be insufficient for development of economic activities considering the special conditions of environment management in the BNA.

The amendment of the list of activities prohibited within the CEZ in the BNA, which took place in 2014, improves the environment for promoting environmental business in the RB. Further promotion of environmentally non-damaging economic activities in the BNA, however, is necessary along with widening the scope of the system of payment for ecosystem services (PES).

Outline of measures

1. Set support to environment-oriented activities in the BNA as a priority of the RB's socio-economic development.

Environment-oriented activities in the BNA should be included in the legal acts of the RB setting the priorities of socio-economic development of the region (the RB law "On a Programme of Socio-Economic Development of the Republic of Buryatia till 2020", #1903-IV, 14 March 2011, etc.). Within the framework of the project, a preliminary list of relevant activities appears below:

- ecotourism and other types of tourism that respect undisturbed natural areas
- production of bottled Baikal water
- collection and use of wild-growing herbs
- production of ecologically "clean" products without using pesticides, herbicides, synthetic fertilisers and growth-promoting substance
- use of alternative sources of energy
- environmental auditing and advising services
- creation of research-and-education centres, laboratories and research-and-production complexes for development and testing of new environment-oriented technologies
- widening the scope of the system of PES.

2. Streamline regulations concerning state support for environment-oriented activities in the BNA through the following changes:

- Amend the RB's laws and regulations to extend state support to environment-oriented investment projects in the form of state guarantees of the RB, tax benefits, investment tax credits and leases of the RB's state property on attractive terms or as a guarantee:
  - RB law "On state support for investment activities on the territory of the RB" (#868-IV, 8 May 2009)
  - RB law "On selected issues of tax regulation in the RB assigned to the Constituent Subjects of the RF by the RF Taxation and Revenue Law" (#145-III, 26 November 2002)
- Amending the RB law "On public-private partnership in the RB" (#2625-IV, 16 March 2012) by way of including environment-oriented activities to the concept of "projects of public importance".

3. Assign an authorised body of the RB with responsibilities relating to state support to environment-oriented activities.

Estimated incremental cost and fiscal effect

The measures may be implemented as part of the routine work of public authorities with no incremental costs. The effects should be estimated for each project.

Implementing the measures: level of authority and relationship with the Russian Federation's water policy

Implementation of the measures outlined in Table 5.4 requires actions by regional bodies of state power, with focus on enhancing the efficiency of WRM in the BNA.

Table 5.4. **"Implementability" and estimated period of implementation**

Measure	"Implementability"	Period of implementation	
		Based on the scope of work	Taking into account political, social and economic acceptability
Strengthening support to environment-oriented activities as a priority of socio-economic development in the RB	Moderate	3-6 months	3-6 months
Streamlining regulations concerning state support to environment-oriented activities in the BNA		1-2 years	1-3 years
Assigning an authorised body of the RB with responsibilities relating to state support to environment-oriented activities		1-2 years	3-4 years

Source: Authors' recommendations and estimates.

The interrelated measures shall be implemented as presented.

Expected outcome

- More conducive legal environment and organisational conditions and stronger economic incentives for environment-oriented activities in the BNA.

5.5. Introduction of payment for ecosystem services

Problem description

Payment for ecosystem services (PES) is an important economic instrument for WRM in international practice (see Box 5.1)

Introduction of PES may become a driving force for protecting and improving the quality of ecosystems. It can have a positive impact on a water management system and environmental management system by creating a flow of funds from the sale of ecosystem services.

Providers of ecosystem services and recipients of revenues generated by PES could be public or private entities. This determines how (for which purposes) the collected revenues (generated by PES) are or could be used, and by whom. Within this context, there are several considerations:

First, if a private agent simply implements measures necessary for full compliance with existing environmental and natural resource management regulation and environmental standards, **such measures could in no way be interpreted as ecosystem services**. Only measures over and above what is needed for full compliance could qualify as an ecosystem service and receive payment. An upstream farmer whose performance is in full compliance with the aforesaid standards and regulations, for example, could take additional measures to improve water quantity and (or) quality downstream by planting bushes and trees on the banks of a stream or river passing its own land spot or by improving pasture practices. This extra effort could qualify as an ecosystem service. This approach helps prevent eventual conflicts between application of the *"polluter pays"* and *"beneficiary pays"* principles.

Box 5.1. **Payment for ecosystem services**

In this project, payment for ecosystem services (PES) is understood as compensation by consumers of ecosystem services (those who benefit from such services) to persons or public entities that own (or control and manage) ecosystem resources. Introduction of PES means the creation of a market for services that were free in the past, but for which the recipients of such services had enjoyed certain economic benefits. The most common ecosystem services relating to WRM include the following:

- supply of quality water
- conservation of biodiversity
- preservation of aesthetic value of landscapes
- carbon-dioxide absorption.

Source : Second interim report under the project (Report # 2).

Second, if private agents (e.g. upstream farmers) provide ecosystem services with their own resources, then payments for these services become taxable revenues to be used at the discretion of the private agents. If public agents or publicly-owned natural resources (ecosystem objects) provide ecosystem services, then revenues from PES would go to the general public budget and (or) dedicated budgetary or extra-budgetary funds that could be earmarked for environment. For example, in the Republic of Buryatia, the payment might be for access to protected natural areas, while collected funds might be spent for environmental purposes.

A combined type of PES is also possible when payment to private agents is combined with payment to the state.

Third, PES should be distinguished from environmental charges – fees, fines, taxes and subsidies. In any case, PES goes beyond creating incentives for implementing environmental measures. It also plays the role of an economic instrument helping to internalise positive externalities. It can generate revenues for the development of environmentally-friendly types of activities and increasing capitalisation of natural resources and of the territory on which they are located.

Presently, in the RB and in the RF overall, provision of ecosystem services is very limited. It is mainly related to the use of specially protected natural areas (SPNAs). At the same time, the RB and Lake Baikal basin have considerable potential for wider application of the scheme. As is the case with other areas of activity, the BNA – with its unique ecosystem and special regulation of environmental management issues – could become a pilot site for the Russian Federation for introduction of PES.

In this regard, international experience of application of PES, such as in the United Kingdom, might serve as a good example (see Report # 2).

Outline of measures

A dedicated assessment and evaluation of natural capital of Lake Baikal's ecosystem will identify types of ecosystem services relating to WRM in respect to Lake Baikal basin. A list of the relevant measures should be prepared that gives due consideration for a concept based on special research (see sub-section 2.3.1). Within the scope of the present recommendations, the following areas have been identified:

1. Establish (increase) and streamline payments for the use of natural resources, and, specifically:

- Introduce admission charges for visiting SPNA (including vehicle admission charges and parking charges). This requires developing a tolling scheme to collect the funds needed to cover the costs incurred by SPNA and providers of ecosystem services with the aim of conserving biodiversity, protecting and restoring the ecosystems.
- Mobilise funds through introduction of a "resort fee" charged to each visitor per 24 hours of stay in the protected natural area.

2. Introduce a system of voluntary agreements between private entrepreneurs and the RB government to regulate cost recovery relating to environmental protection and conservation of biodiversity.

3. Create a dedicated (ear-marked) fund for accumulating some portion of revenues from payment for ecosystem services to develop the RB's water sector and Lake Baikal basin.

One option consists in accumulating the proceeds in a dedicated fund for support to the BNA (a state corporation, see sub-section 2.5.2). If a state corporation is not created, an alternative solution is needed to secure the targeted use of funds for conservation of the ecosystem of Lake Baikal.

4. Compile a list of ecosystem services that might be provided or are already in place on the territory of the Republic of Buryatia, in particular on the BNA. In addition, develop a system of preliminary economic and monetary evaluation of the natural capital of the BNA. Its components should be ranked, and priorities identified, for use, capitalisation and development, starting with the most valuable ones.

Estimated incremental cost and fiscal effect

Relevant estimates require special research and analysis that are beyond the scope of the project.

Implementing the measures: level of authority and relationship with the Russian Federation's water policy

Implementation of Measure 1 requires actions by federal authorities. Regional authorities (adjusting action in the region to reflect federal efforts) have power to implement other measures aimed at improving efficiency of WRM in the BNA (see Table 5.5). Measures should be implemented both in the RB and Irkutsk Oblast. The recommended measures may be implemented independently.

Table 5.5. **"Implementability" and estimated period of implementation**

Measure	"Implementability"	Period of implementation	
		Based on the scope of work	Taking into account political, social and economic acceptability
Establishing (increasing) and adjusting charges for use of natural resources	Moderate	1-2 years	2-3 years
Introducing a system of voluntary agreements between private entrepreneurs and the RB government to regulate cost recovery relating to environmental protection and conservation of biodiversity	Low	2-3 years	2-3 years
Creating a dedicated fund for charging and accumulating part of payment for ecosystem services for the development of the RB's water sector and Lake Baikal Basin	Moderate	2-3 years	2-3 years

Source: Authors' recommendations and estimates.

Expected outcome

- much wider use of payment for ecosystem services within the BNA and increased financing of environmental measures funded from the proceeds
- further development of SPNA through promotion of additional fundraising measures and contribution to conservation of biodiversity.

5.6. Redistribution of hydro-energy rent and introduction of a mechanism of compensation for environmental damage caused to the Baikal ecosystem and to the economy of coastal districts

Problem description

In the 1960s, a hydro-energy cascade was built on the Angara River that which draining from Lake Baikal. The location provided the opportunity for large amounts of cheap electric power because of favourable weather conditions (high flow of water, steep drop in the Angara River, high natural storage capacity of Lake Baikal and convenience of individual dam sites). The cost of power production, however, by no means takes into account the damage caused to the ecosystem of Lake Baikal and to the economy of coastal areas (to economic agents and activities) i.e. respective negative externalities have never been internalised.

Construction of a cascade of hydro-electric stations (HES) on the Angara River changed the lake's water flow regime. Specifically, the average long-standing level of water table in the lake increased by 1.2 metres. This readjustment has had enormous detrimental effect on the ecosystem of Lake Baikal, and on the nature and economy of its coastal area (increased incidence of floods and mud flows in some areas of the RB). The most significant damage was caused to water ecosystems and areas in the eastern lowland coast within the boundaries of the RB. Thus, Irkutsk Oblast and the economic agents operating within its territory appear to be the major beneficiaries of the HES operations, while the RB mainly bears losses. It does not even benefit from supply of the cheap electricity produced by the HES, due to poor linkages with the electricity network of Irkutsk Oblast and high costs of transportation. Instead, electricity is produced locally with much higher unit costs at thermal power plants.

As a result, despite the use of Lake Baikal for hydro energy production, electricity tariff rates in the RB are very high. In 2015, the electricity tariff rate – based on a single-rate (by volume) tariff for domestic users (households) – ranged from RUB 2.9-4.3 per kilowatt hour in the RB; it was five-six times higher than in Irkutsk Oblast where domestic tariffs varied from RUB 0.5-0.9 per kilowatt hour.

In summary, the high electricity tariff rates in the RB is likely because of high cost of transporting electric power from Irkutsk Oblast to Buryatia, insufficient capacity and low efficiency of transforming substations, and high costs of on-site generating capacities in the RB (mostly thermal power stations using fossil fuels). In any case, high tariffs for electric power in the RB indirectly contribute to higher pollution of Lake Baikal and impair competitive capacity of the RB in power-intensive activities. Electricity expenses make up a considerable portion of production costs of water utilities whereas biological treatment is energy intensive. Due to their deteriorated financial position, water utilities are not always able to pay electricity bills. To reduce the bill, they may have to limit wastewater treatment to mechanical treatment only).

In the late 2000s, hydro-energy rent – the share appropriated by Irkutsk Oblast – was successfully redistributed: on the basis of a special agreement, Irkutsk Oblast regularly transferred a proportion of appropriated rent to the RB's public budget. The scheme was abolished, however, after an amendment to the relevant federal law (see Report #1).

Re-establishing the mechanism for redistribution of hydro-energy rent would – at least partly – compensate for damage to the ecosystem of Lake Baikal and coastal areas, and help improve WRM in the BNA. Parameters for the future compensation mechanism and selection of appropriate economic instruments for implementation require special research.

Outline of measures

1. Refine the methodology for assessing damage from the negative impact of hydro-energy industry on the ecosystem of Lake Baikal, the economics and population of coastal areas through the following:

- Assess damage caused to aquatic biological resources after a streamflow regulation occurs (due to seasonal fluctuations of water table levels in the lake, and in periods of excessive water flow).
- Assess economic damage caused by water-related hazards: floods, destruction of banks hollowed out by waves and rushing waters, etc.

2. Update guidelines on calculation of the amount, appropriation and adequate redistribution of hydro-energy rent arising from use of water resources of Lake Baikal for hydro-energy.

There are various ways to estimate the amount of economic benefits:

- Calculations take into account extra (incremental) production of electric power because of a changed level of the water table of Lake Baikal: economic benefits are estimated as incremental net income from the volume of extra production of electric power at the Angara HES cascade (by comparing the volumes of production in case of the natural level of water table in Lake Baikal and at the changed level).

- **Calculation procedures take into account the total volume of production of electric power**: economic benefits are estimated as the product of *(a)* the total volume of production of electric power at the Angara HES cascade by *(b)* the difference of average cost of production of electric power by the region's thermal stations and the cost of electric power produced by the Angara HES cascade.

According to available scientific research, suitable schemes for appropriation and redistribution of hydro-energy rent are as follows:

- **Water-area approach**: in proportion to the share of the RB (62.4%) in the total water area of Lake Baikal.
- **Compensatory approach**: in proportion to the damage caused by construction of hydro-energy facilities to a part of water area, and costs of Lake Baikal within the boundaries of the RB (accounting for the share of RB in the total area of flooded land (this indicator was previously estimated at 95.7%).

There are other ways to calculate the amount and recommended redistribution of hydro-energy rent. Further in-depth research is required to select the best scheme.

3. Introduce **a sound mechanism of compensation** for damage caused to the ecosystem of Lake Baikal and the economy of the coastal areas from using water resources from the lake for hydro energy production. A special tax (charge) on production of electric power could be used. The tax rate should take into account all electric energy production costs, including environmental and resource costs.

International practice demonstrates that the redistributed rent could be used for a special purpose. In this regard, the creation of a special purpose fund could be an option (see sub-section 2.5.2). The designated (earmarked) use of redistributed rent should also be considered. For instance, part of the rent should be used for providing electric energy to the population and the economy of the RB at affordable prices, not least through strengthening the system links (high-voltage grids, transforming stations) with the energy system of Irkutsk Oblast.

Estimated incremental cost and fiscal effect

Accurate estimates require special research and analysis that are beyond the scope of the project.

Implementing the measures: level of authority and relationship with the Russian Federation's water policy

The measures presented in Table 5.6 seek to enhance the efficiency of WRM in the BNA; the implementation requires actions by federal authorities. The recommended measures could be replicated by other regions of the RF facing similar situations with the use of trans-boundary water resources (e.g. Yenisei HES cascade and Volga-Kama HES cascade, etc.).

Table 5.6. **"Implementability" and estimated period of implementation**

Measure	"Implementability"	Period of implementation	
		Based on the scope of work	Taking into account political, social and economic acceptability
Refining the methodology to assess damage from the negative impact of the hydro-energy industry on the ecosystem of Lake Baikal, the economics and population of the coastal areas	Low	1-3 years	1-3 years
Updating methodological guidelines on calculation of the amount and adequate redistribution of rent from use of water resources of Lake Baikal by the hydro-energy industry		1-3 years	1-3 years
Introducing a mechanism of compensation for damage caused to the ecosystem of Lake Baikal and the economics of the coastal areas from using the lake for hydro energy production		2-3 years	5-7 years

Source: Authors' recommendations and estimates.

The measures are interrelated. Measures 1 and 2 should be implemented prior to Measure 3.

Expected outcome

- compensation for damage caused to the ecosystem of Lake Baikal and the economy of the coastal areas because of changes made to the hydrology of the lake by producers of hydropower downstream
- introduction of a system to internalise full environmental and water resource costs in the cost on electric energy produced by the Angara HES cascade, complemented by pricing to fully cover all production costs
- receipt of funds by the RB from redistribution of the hydro-energy rent, and designated (earmarked) use of the relevant funds.

If proved economically viable, *the adjusted compensation mechanism could be applied in respect of trans-boundary systems*. Export of electric energy to Mongolia, at steady and attractive prices, could be exchanged for Mongolia's commitment to abandon its plans to build an HES in the upper reaches of the Selenga River – the main confluent of Lake Baikal – since the plans could cause considerable damage to water resources and the ecosystem of Lake Baikal.

However, economic agents and regional authorities participating in redistribution of hydro-energy rent *may want to maximise benefits even at the cost of damage to Lake Baikal and its ecosystem*. In order to prevent such damage, fluctuations in the lake's water table should be kept within limits close to natural values observed and known for generations. This concern is reflected in the recommendation below.

5.7. Facilitation of efforts aiming to ensure that fluctuations of water level in Lake Baikal are close to their natural values

Problem description

The level of Lake Baikal depends on natural factors (relationship of surface water flows and groundwater flows, on precipitation in the lake's catchment area and on evaporation), as well as from the relationship between the Angara and Yenisei HES cascades. The former has a profound negative effect on the ecosystem of the BNA and Lake Baikal, as well as on the economy of its coastal areas in the part of the BNA located within the boundaries of the RB (see sub-section 2.3.6).

Beginning in 2001, water levels in the lake have fluctuated within limits established by the RF government (i.e. between 456-457 m above the Baltic Sea level). In recent years, however, the negative impact of the Angara HES cascade has been growing. In 2012-15, *Boguchansk* HES (the fourth HES of the cascade) was commissioned. Today, the feasibility of building *Nizhneangarsk* HES (the fifth HES of the cascade) is under discussion. As of the beginning of 2015, water level of Lake Baikal had dropped almost to the minimum acceptable level of water at 456 m.

The increasingly intense use of the lake's water resources for hydro energy causes stronger fluctuations of water levels. This has led to strained relationships between the bodies of public power, operators of the Angara HES cascade in Irkutsk Oblast and environmental organisations.

At the same time, irrespective of any particular phase of multiyear flow, annual water variations in Lake Baikal must be returned to natural values observed before construction of the HES. This objective is also envisaged by federal documents setting the priorities for WRM in the BNA.

According to most experts involved, and representatives of hydro-energy companies, public authorities and NGOs, the regulation of the lake's water level should rely on well-grounded and duly approved guidelines. The relevant regulations should take into account the total impact of the Angara HES cascade on Lake Baikal drawing on in-depth research.

A draft "Rules for the use of water resources of water reservoirs of Angara HES cascade" was also prepared in this regard. However, as of the beginning of 2015, the above-noted rules have not yet been approved.

Outline of measures

To mitigate the negative impact of the Irkutsk HES on Lake Baikal, the following measures could be considered:

1. Refine and approve "Regulations on the use of water resources of Lake Baikal and water storage reservoirs of the Angara HES cascade".

This measure assumes that the Federal Agency for Water Resources approves the regulations, which should envisage changing the operating parameters of the HES cascade to obtain values of annual water table variations in Lake Baikal close to natural ones. **Uniform regulations** must be approved rather than individual rules for every water storage reservoir.

2. Develop and approve regulations for managing water levels of Lake Baikal, and water levels and streamflow at the lower pool of the Irkutsk HES under conditions of excessive

water flow. Regulations should also be approved by the Federal Agency for Water Resources to regulate water table levels in the lake under conditions of excessive water flow.

3. Develop a system to monitor responses of the aquatic and coastal ecosystems to changes in water table levels in Lake Baikal, as a result of external situations, and use results for adjusting "Regulations on the use of water resources of Lake Baikal and water storage reservoirs of the Angara HES cascade". To that end, a list of biological indicators should be prepared, and the values of indicators determined systematically. The system should be developed as part of the general system of state environmental monitoring of Lake Baikal (see sub-section 2.5.1).

Estimated incremental cost and fiscal effect

The cost of research is estimated at RUB 50-100 million, and the RF budget is most likely to be the source of financing. Assessing impact of the recommended measures on financial position of hydro-energy industry in Irkutsk Oblast necessitates special research and analysis, which are beyond the scope of the present work. Expenditures for implementing Measure 3 could be undertaken as part of development of SEM of Lake Baikal (see sub-section 2.5.1).

Implementing the measures: level of authority and relationship with the Russian Federation's water policy

The measures (Table 5.7) are designed to improve the efficiency of WRM in the BNA; the implementation requires actions by federal authorities.

Table 5.7. **"Implementability" and estimated period of implementation**

Measure	"Implementability"	Period of implementation	
		Based on the scope of work	Taking into account political, social and economic acceptability
Refining and approving "Regulations on the use of water resources of Lake Baikal and water storage reservoirs of the Angara HES cascade"	High	1 year	1 year
Developing and approving the regulations for regulating water levels of Lake Baikal, and water levels and streamflow at the lower pool of the Irkutsk HES under conditions of excessive water flow	High	1-2 years	1-2 years
Developing a system to monitor response of water and coastal ecosystems to water-level changes in Lake Baikal, as a result of extreme situations, and using results for adjusting the "Regulations on the use of water resources of Lake Baikal and water storage reservoirs of the Angara HES cascade"	Moderate	1-2 years	2-3 years

Source: Authors' recommendations and estimates.

Measures 1 and 2 appear to be interrelated and, hence, should be carried out as presented. Measure 3 could be implemented independently (except for taking into account the results of monitoring when adjusting the regulations).

Expected outcome

- water storage reservoirs of the Angara HES cascade operate in a manner most favourable for the ecosystems of Lake Baikal and the economy of coastal areas
- the water table level in Lake Baikal is maintained at 456-457 m (over the Baltic Sea level), as provided for in the RF government decree
- the negative impact of changes in water table level in Lake Baikal is monitored, with due consideration for biological indicators and prompt regulation of the Angara HES cascade, if and when needed.

References

Government of the Russian Federation, Decree "On Federal Target Programme "Protection of Lake Baikal and Socio-Economic Development of the Baikal Natural Area in 2012-2020" (21 August 2012, #847).

Government of the Russian Federation, Decree "On Federal Target Programme "Protection of Lake Baikal and Socio-Economic Development of the Baikal Natural Area in 2012-2020" (21 August 2012, #847).

Federal Law "On Environmental Impact Assessment" (#174-ФЗ, 23 November 1995).

RB law "On a Programme of Socio-Economic Development of the Republic of Buryatia till 2020", #1903-IV, 14 March 2011.

RB law "On state support for investment activities on the territory of the RB" (#868-IV, 8 May 2009).

RB law "On selected issues of tax regulation in the RB assigned to the Constituent Subjects of the RF by the RF Taxation and Revenue Law" (#145-III, 26 November 2002).

RB law "On public-private partnership in the RB" (#2625-IV, 16 March 2012).

Chapter 6

Enhancement of instruments for improving the efficiency of water supply and sanitation and irrigation systems in Buryatia

Two key recommendations are presented in this chapter:

– streamlining tariff policy in the WSS sector; and

– facilitation of introduction of charges for irrigation of agricultural land, including payment for water as natural resource.

6.1. Streamlining tariff policy in the WSS sector

Problem description

An important principle of WRM is full recovery of costs incurred by a water utility company. This includes operational and capital costs, energy costs, and environmental and resource costs. The RB established cheap tariffs for WSS services without accounting for actual replacement cost of fixed assets relating to WSS. About two-thirds of costs incurred by water supply companies in the RB are associated with labour costs and energy costs. According to the latest available data, costs for maintenance, ordinary repairs and a major overhaul made up only 5% of total production costs of WSS companies, while depreciation costs were estimated at a mere 2%. Considering significant physical depreciation and high rate of breakdowns at the WSS facilities in the RB, overhauls and replacement of fixed assets of the WSS facilities were seriously underfunded. This fact notwithstanding, state support to WSS in the republic appears to be scarce; in recent years, it has covered less than 1% of all the costs incurred by WSS companies.

Analysis presented in Report #1 detected room for increasing the tariffs. More recently, household expenditure for WSS has made up about 1% of average per capita income. That is, it is two times below the lowest threshold of WSS affordability to the population applied by international organisations, particularly the European Bank for Reconstruction and Development (EBRD).

Providing sufficient funding also encompasses an objective of selecting an appropriate tariff structure. The RB applies volume-based tariffs for WSS services. **Absence of cross-subsidisation** is an advantage of the existing tariff system. International practice of WRM, however, suggests that introduction of two-part tariffs – that combined a fixed payment and a volume component – should be carefully considered. Indeed, accurately determined two-part tariffs would encourage users to save water, and simultaneously ensure financial sustainability of service providers. Eventual impact on vulnerable households could and should be addressed through targeted social support measures.

Outline of measures

1. Increase WSS tariffs and/or strengthen state support to WSS companies. Given federal constraints to the growth of combined payments for housing and utility services by households, funding of WSS enterprises might be increased in one of the following ways:

- Establish higher maximum indices for WSS tariffs increase (giving consideration for special status of the RB's water sector among the RF regions).
- Mobilise additional funds through direct state financing of projects and/or via compensating lost profits (due to low tariff rates that fail to cover the cost of needed renewal of fixed assets of WSS enterprises in the RB).

In spite of the potential for increasing tariffs, political considerations mean any increase is unlikely in the short term. Additional direct state financing also appears to be unlikely due to the difficult fiscal situation.

2. Introduce two-part tariffs for WSS services in the RB, which means use of rates listed below:

1. A rate (a fixed monthly subscriber fee) for maintenance of centralised cold water supply systems or centralised sanitation systems, or for maintenance of facilities relating to the above systems (a rate of charge for maintenance of capacities).

2. A rate for the volume of water consumed (supplied by the centralised water supply system), or for the volume of wastewater discharged into sewerage network, respectively.

Estimated incremental cost and fiscal effect

A required minimum growth of tariffs for WSS services is estimated at 40-60%. This would generate about RUB 480-720 million of extra user charge revenues per year, in respect to WS services, in 2014 prices. If tariff rates did increase, compensation to vulnerable households from the public budget (at the expense of state funds) would amount to at least one-third of the additional user charge revenues (i.e. some RUB 160-240 million). Most likely, the funds required for support to WSS would be allocated by federal authorities.

Implementing the measures: level of authority and relationship with the Russian Federation's water policy

The measures (Table 6.1) aim at enhancing the efficiency of WRM in the BNA. Implementation of Measure 1 (development of legal framework) requires actions by federal authorities while regional authorities should follow with specific tariff decisions and state funding decisions. Implementation of Measure 2 requires actions by the RB's regional bodies of state power.

Table 6.1. **"Implementability" and estimated period of implementation**

Measure	"Implementability"	Period of implementation	
		Based on the scope of work	Taking into account political, social and economic acceptability
Increasing WSS tariffs and/or strengthening state support to WSS companies	Low	1 year	2-3 years
Introducing two-part tariffs for WSS services in the RB	Moderate	1 year	2-3 years

Source: Authors' recommendations and estimates.

The recommended measures may be carried out independently of one another.

Expected outcome

- increased investments funded from user change revenues of WSS enterprises up to, at least, the average national level (i.e. from 11-18%)
- opportunity for forming and financing the investment programmes of WSS enterprises that focus on renewal of worn-out or highly deteriorated fixed assets
- incentives for water saving, while providing adequate financial flows to WSS enterprises.

6.2. Facilitation of introduction of charges for irrigation of agricultural land

Problem description

Key problems associated with irrigation in the RB consist of highly deteriorated irrigation systems, and acute underfunding of development and rehabilitation of these systems, as well as of their normal operation and maintenance. The financing gap leads to further degradation of irrigation systems.

The relevant projects are funded mainly from the federal budget. Revenue from irrigation charges tends to be insignificant compared to the amount of state financing and considering actual financial needs for maintenance of irrigation systems (see Report #1). Federal legislation establishes that **the service provided by systems of agricultural land improvement is a supply of water, whereas payments for water as a resource are not applied**. Users (households, farmers and legal entities) are charged only for water supply services. The charges, however, appear to be substantially lower than actual costs of FGBU "*Buryatmelioratzia*", which is responsible for irrigation in the RB.

To make things worse, users often refuse to pay for irrigation water. Cost of irrigation water represents less than 1% in the total cost of agricultural products in the RB. The amount of charges for supply of irrigation water averages at RUB 2 000 per ha in a season, while the average value (market price) of produce is RUB 222 400 per ha (in 2012 market prices). At the same time, in spite of low tariffs, users and heads of rural administrations undermine efforts to improve collection rates. FGBU "*Buryatmelioratzia*" often lacks effective enforcement mechanisms to enable a better collection rate (see Report #1).

Outline of measures

Individual farmers and legal entities should be charged for irrigation **water as a resource**. The policy could be introduced within the RB's regional pilot initiative, with the possibility of replicating the practice in other regions of the Russian Federation. Admittedly, implementing these measures requires substantial administrative effort; in the current political economy, it appears to be a politically sensitive and complex task to perform. Despite low probability of implementation, the measure is recommended: in the irrigation sector, in the absence of payment for surface water as a natural resource, the incentives are distorted in the eyes of water users (because of unaccountable and non-economic water use).

The following measures are needed to introduce payments for water as a resource for irrigation needs:

1. Select the RB as a pilot region for introduction of payments for water as a resource for irrigation needs.

2. Provide legal framework for introduction of payments for water as a resource for irrigation needs, as this relates to the RB:

- Amend federal laws to introduce payment for irrigation water as a natural resource.
- Give regional authorities the responsibility for setting tariffs for use of water for irrigation needs.
- Issue a joint order (by the Ministry of Natural Resources and Environmental Protection of the RF and the Ministry of Agriculture of the RF) establishing a procedure for calculation of rates and determining the amount of payments for irrigation water as a resource.

As is evident from international practice (see Report #2), there are two baseline options for determining and setting payments for water as a resource. Both cubic metres of water (a volume-based method) and hectares of irrigated area may be used to calculate charges for irrigation water as natural resource. A combined option of **a two-part tariff** for irrigation water is also possible. The tariff would consider the price of water as a resource and the costs of water supply infrastructure services (abstraction and supply of water for irrigation and other needs in agriculture). A two-part tariff is recommended for the long run.

3. Implement a pilot project in the RB for water charges based on two-part tariffs. This would involve calculating tariff rates, introducing a system to measure the volume of irrigation water supplied and raising public awareness.

Considering the increased financial burden on agricultural producers, more effective support measures to agricultural industry are needed (e.g. support to developing rural roads, labs for certification and infrastructure for storage of agricultural products). At the same time, agricultural land improvement and increased charges for water and supply of irrigation water should be considered in the context of development of rural areas and agriculture. These recommendations do not focus on **measures promoting support to rural areas and agriculture** because the subject is outside the scope of the project. As is evident from international practice, however, in terms of rural and agricultural development, several alternative measures **often turn out to be much more cost-effective, in practice, than support through reduced charges for irrigation water**. These include: developing road infrastructure and WSS systems in rural areas; establishing a system of certification agricultural products, including for export; developing infrastructure for storage and processing of agricultural products; and supporting co-operative systems of farming.

4. Strengthen administrative responsibility for failure to pay for supply of irrigation water, and, in case of implementation of Measures 1-3, for failure to pay for water as a resource.

Estimated incremental cost and fiscal effect

Effect from the recommended measures for the RB could be estimated only after a decision is made about changing procedures for charging. The parameters should be determined following special analysis, which is not envisaged within the scope of the report.

Implementing the measures: level of authority and relationship with the Russian Federation's water policy

Measures (Table 6.2) within the pilot project aim at enhancing the efficiency of WRM in the BNA. Measure 4 is a general component of RF water policy. Implementation of the first stage of Measure 1 (development of legal framework) requires actions by federal authorities while regional authorities should follow up. The solutions could be replicated in other regions of the RF later on.

Table 6.2. **"Implementability" and estimated period of implementation**

Measure	"Implementability"	Period of implementation	
		Based on the scope of work	Taking into account political, social and economic acceptability
Determining the RB as a pilot region for introduction of payments for irrigation water as a resource	Low	2-3 years	4-5 years
Providing legal framework for introduction of payments for irrigation water as a resource as related to the RB			
Implementing a pilot project in the RB with the aim of introducing two-part water tariffs			
Strengthening the administrative responsibility for failure to pay for irrigation water consumed	Moderate	1 year	1 year

Source: Authors' recommendations and estimates.

Measures 1-3 appear to be interrelated. Hence, these should be implemented in the order presented above. Measure 4 might be implemented independently.

Expected outcome

- sufficient financing for adequate operation, maintenance and rehabilitation of irrigation systems in the RB
- economic incentives to encourage a more efficient use of irrigation water
- dissemination of the practice of payments for water as a resource used for irrigation needs to other regions of the Russian Federation.

Chapter 7

Enhancing state support to the water sector in Buryatia

State support to the water sector in Buryatia and the Baikal Natural Area (BNA) could be drastically improved focusing on cost-effective measures while reforming or phasing out existing counter-productive instruments. From this perspective, the following recommendations are made in this chapter:

– introduce regulatory impact assessment (RIA) on a routine basis;

– partially reallocate federal funds from budget subsidies, to budget equalisation transfers (grants), and increased allocations for the latter;

– strengthen the revenue base of local governments;

– establish a dedicated fund for support to the BNA; and

– the use of public funds to support implementation of wastewater treatment technologies to enable the attainment of standards for quality of water objects located within the BNA, as well as the development of storm water collector-drainage systems, on-site sanitation to reduce and clean-up discharges of liquid domestic waste and wastewater into Lake Baikal.

7.1. Raising cost-effectiveness of state support to the water sector in the RB and the BNA

Problem description

In general, state policy to support the water sector and the BNA is carried out in accordance with general provisions in federal legislation. The existing system of state support envisages target financing of measures and investment expenditures. If compared with relevant good international practice, however, the Russian system lacks flexibility.[1] Most federal funds are granted to the RB water sector in the form of subsidies and subventions (target transfers spent strictly according to designated purposes). Given that federal authorities have primary responsibility for the sector, regional and local governments are often unable to respond promptly to changes and to select the most efficient solutions with consideration for expert knowledge of the local environment.

The most crucial problem of state policy, as it applies to the RB and the BNA, is that federal authorities did not take responsibility for the economic impact of their decisions. Another acute problem is that present regulation of environmental management and nature conservation in the BNA results in uncompensated heavy economic losses for the region. The state should have considered the impact of the above-mentioned constraints on its system of support to the water sector.

In addition, municipal authorities play a minor part in decision-making as it relates to the public sector. In general, local governments merely execute decisions taken at federal and regional levels and financed from inter-budget transfers. Financial and organisational weakness of municipal authorities appears to be a common problem in the RF.[2] Regional governance in the RB is also facing the same problem.

Outline of measures

1. Envisage in law "On Protection of Lake Baikal" and assess, on a regular basis, the regulatory impact of the law and bylaws on the regions relating to the BNA (the Republic of Buryatia, Irkutsk Oblast, the *Zabaikalski Krai*).

Regulatory impact assessment (RIA) would help prepare official cost estimates of economic losses suffered by constituents of the RF, where the BNA is located, from specific federal requirements, bans on and constraints related to many economic activities in the BNA. Results of the RIA should be considered when determining the amount of inter-budget transfers from the RF to the RB. Results of the assessment should be regularly revised with consideration for changed socio-economic conditions in the BNA and the RF federal law.

2. A partial shift in the use of federal funds from budget subsidies, allocated for support to the BNA, to budget equalisation transfers (grants), and increased allocations for the latter.

Regional bodies of state power in the RB have responsibility for determining the designated use of budget equalisation transfers, which is not the case for budget subsidies. A partial use of budget equalisation transfers is recommended to provide regional authorities with more opportunity for self-reliance. At the same time, targeted funds in the form of subsidies shall be provided to finance the most important projects on the BNA.

3. Strengthen the revenue base of local governments for most effective performance of responsibilities relating to WRM.

The strengthening of a revenue base shall take place in respect of all the municipalities within the RF. This measure implies amending the RF Tax Code and the RF Budget Code. Among other measures, they can **introduce a resort fee in the BNA** (and distribute respective revenues between municipalities of the BNA and a dedicated fund for support to the BNA – see sub-section 2.5.2), as well as use of an adjustment factor in regard to land tax and individual property tax (see sub-section 2.6.3). Reassigning additional tax revenue (specifically, additional standard shares of the personal income tax) from local budgets to regional ones should also be considered.

Apart from the above-mentioned measures, the system of state support to the RF water sector might be improved by creating a dedicated fund for project financing in the BNA (see sub-section 2.5.2).

The measures should be carried out within the entire BNA, including Irkutsk Oblast.

Estimated incremental cost and fiscal effect

The shift from budget subsidies to equalisation transfers should make use of results of the RIA for determining the amount and proportions, and increase allocations from the federal budget. By a very preliminary expert estimation, the annual amount of equalisation transfers could be RUB 2-2.5 billion (in 2014 prices) based on the following factors: the estimated losses of the RB at 5-7% of the GRP (due to federal bans on and constraints to some economic activities in the RB (see Report#1); the RB's GRP of RUB 183.8 billion (2013); and the resulting tax burden on the economy as this relates to taxes assigned to regional and local budgets (about 10%). The RUB 2.-2.5 billion transfer could be allocated in the following way (preliminary expert estimation):

- RUB 0.9-1.2 billion – to supplement current public financing (compensation of economic losses caused to the BNA)
- RUB 1-1.5 billion transferred in the form of grants that were previously assigned as budget subsidies.

In the short run, the probability of accomplishing the measure appears to be low for two reasons: the substantial amount of funds required; and the break from previous methods and practice of development of budget legislation.

Implementing the measures: level of authority and relationship with the Russian Federation's water policy

Implementation of the measures outlined in Table 7.1 requires actions by federal authorities. The recommended measures may be implemented independently.

Measures 1-2, in the form recommended, seek to improve the efficiency of WRM in the BNA. In the long run, similar measures might also be implemented to support other regions, territories and water objects. Measure 3 shall be carried out in respect of all the municipalities in the RF.

Table 7.1. **"Implementability" and estimated period of implementation**

Measure	"Implementability"	Period of implementation	
		Based on the scope of work	Taking into account political, social and economic acceptability
Envisaging in law "On Protection of Lake Baikal" and assessing, on a regular basis, the regulatory impact assessment of the law and bylaws on regions relating to the BNA	Low	1-2 years	2-3 years
Partial shift in the use of federal funds from budget subsidies to the BNA, to budget equalisation transfers, and increased allocations for the latter transfers	Low	1-2 years	2-3 years
Strengthening revenue base of local governments for most effective performance of responsibilities relating to WRM	Low	1-2 years	2-3 years

Source: Authors' recommendations and estimates.

Expected outcome

- annual assessment of regulatory impact of federal regulatory framework establishing requirements for performance of economic activities and other activities in the BNA
- increased federal financing in regard to the RB, foremost in the form of annual equalisation transfers from the federal budget to the RB's budget
- improved fiscal capacity and self-sufficiency (degree of financial autonomy), and sustainability of municipal budgets, in the RB and the RF.

7.2. Establishing a dedicated fund for support to the BNA

Problem description

As mentioned in sub-section 2.5.1, the current system of state support to the RF water sector relies on general provisions of federal legislation and appears to be inflexible. The RF Budget Code almost eliminates the possibility of targeted use of public funds in the form of taxes and charges (this concerns all sectors, not only the water sector).

International practice in applying economic instruments for WRM, however, proves the feasibility of creating dedicated funds (budget, extra-budget and non-budget funds) to support the water sector. Establishing the funds would accomplish a significant number of policy objectives; ensure minimum volume of financing each year; and ensure stability of funding for important **long-term policy objectives** (the major objectives of support to the BNA cannot be attained within an elected officer's time in office, or within the period of implementing federal target programmes). Another good practice, mostly attainable through target financing, consists in adjusting regulatory effects of economic instruments and the relevant gains (see Report #2).

The problem of mobilising sufficient funds for water infrastructure might also be solved with the help of a dedicated fund because its activities cannot be affected by budget changes. Among key problems facing the RF economy is low availability of long-term credit and finance for water at an acceptable cost. In the BNA, this problem stands in the way of water management companies, and other water users and polluters of water resources; it impedes their switching to more environment-friendly (and, typically) less resource-consuming technologies. International practice proves that effective state policy involves direct lending to organisations in the water sector on non-market conditions, or on concessional, easy terms (in particular cases, with partial debt forgiveness). Current RF legislation prohibits direct lending of public funds to economic entities from budget funds. In this connection, introduction of direct lending necessitates creation of a separate agency. The agency's performance should be regulated by special legislation rather than general provisions of public law.

Outline of measures

With a view to enhancing a system of state support as it relates to the BNA, **a dedicated fund for support to the BNA** – entitled to its own revenue sources and spending responsibilities – could be set up. Considering the objectives of the above agency and legal organisational forms in the RF, **the fund could be established as a state corporation (SC).** In the RF, SC is an autonomous non-profit entity based on asset contribution by the RF, which performs specific social or management functions, or other functions of public importance.

General operational principles of a state corporation are provided for in Federal Law "On Non-Profit Organisations" (#7-ФЗ, dated 12 January 1996). A dedicated federal law for each state corporation (SC) is required to specify its mandate. SCs may be entitled make laws. Although existing SCs are not entitled to accumulate taxes and charges, it seems to be an attainable function (as distinct from joint-stock companies and other economic entities).

So, the legal and organisational form of SC is believed to be more flexible and efficient than other available alternatives allowed by Russian law. It is more flexible than, say, creation of a special purpose government body, as it allows for accumulation and ear-marked use of funds. At the same time, SC is a structure under government control; hence, it can participate effectively in the law making and budgetary processes.

The recommended type of SC presents an effective "organisational envelope" for an array of other measures offered in this report. The recommendations, hence, contain only those measures that relate to creation of the SC, and a separately outlined measure to support the water sector by extending soft loans on a competitive basis.

1. Establish a state corporation called "The Fund for Support to the Baikal Natural Area", and provide legislative, organisational and financial support to it. Such an SC implies the passing of a federal law, asset contribution from the RF budget and an organisational structure and managerial body. This managerial body should be linked to the Inter-Agency Commission for Protection of Lake Baikal.

Budget: the recommended SC would form its budget from the funds outlined below:

- Asset contribution of the RF to the authorised capital of the SC (made as a lump-sum or a regular payment).
- Rent from the use of water resources of Lake Baikal for production of electric power by the Angara HES cascade (a proportion of the rent appropriated by Irkutsk Oblast – see sub-section 2.3.6). Relevant payments should be accumulated entirely in the SC.
- Transfers from federal, regional and municipal budgets relating to the territories where the BNA is located. Among others, the transfers should also include a proportion

of revenue received from resort fee (approximately 30-50% of the collected tax revenues),[3] and revenue from a charge (tax) on toxic agrochemicals and on synthetic detergents used in the BNA) (see sub-section 2.2.4).

Additionally, the SC's budget might receive part of the proceeds from ecosystem services provided in the RB by publicly-owned ecosystems[4] (while complying, in this regard, with specially established requirements).

A list of sources for financing a dedicated fund for support to the BNA should be prepared based on special research.

Main activities (designated use of funds) of the SC might be as follows:

- facilitating the modernisation and development of the water sector by extending soft loans to respective projects and actions on a competitive basis
- financing projects relating to collection, transportation and safe disposal of household waste generated in the BNA (see sub-section 2.2.5)
- financing projects to develop environment-oriented activities (see sub-section 2.3.4)
- financing environmental measures, including treatment of wastewater and rehabilitation of water resources damaged as a result of economic activities in the past.

Sources of revenue and areas of spending are not limited to those specified above, and may be supplemented in the process of SC and WRM development.

2. Assign the SC with the responsibility for development of a system of support to the water sector in the form of soft loans extended on a competitive basis.

The proposed scheme should enhance the affordability of long-term loans extended on attractive terms, and, in certain cases, provide for allocation of funds on a non-repayable basis (e.g. support to "green" components of the project). It is recommended to extend support mainly to WSS companies and other polluters of water resources. The system of support is supposed to be project-oriented to ensure accurate estimates of costs and benefits related to, and produced by, relevant projects and companies.

In light of international practice of similar agencies, special emphasis should be given to the following issues while extending support:

- provision of funds on a competitive basis where feasible (evaluating bids submitted by sponsors of projects that qualify for receiving the funds)
- flexibility of procedures for loans and altering lending terms and conditions in response to changes of key factors in the operational environment of a borrower
- long-term assessment of socio-economic and environmental impact of projects, assessment of situation during implementation or in case of a failure to do so[5]
- promotion of inter-municipal co-operation in regard to implementation of projects with the aim of achieving economies of scale and improving economic efficiency of projects.

In establishing and supporting the operation of the SC "The Fund for Support to the Baikal Natural Area", it also might be advisable to consider the experience obtained by the SC "The Housing and Utilities Reform Fund" established in 2007. In particular, available experience in implementing procedures of extending financial support to legal entities should be reviewed.

Estimated incremental cost and fiscal effect

The minimum annual budget of the SC is estimated at RUB 2-3 billion, in 2014 prices, for the first stage of activities. That amount includes, among other things, budgetary support of the BNA water sector via a competitive tender in the form of soft loans (up to RUB 1 billion). Repayable funds should be paid back from revenues (including, revenue received from charges) of recipient organisations. Funds allocated on a non-repayable basis could be financed only from the RF budgets, and initially from the federal budget. SC activities are expected to increase the rates of growth of GRP and the revenue of consolidated budget of the RF.

Implementing the measures: level of authority and relationship with the Russian Federation's water policy

Implementation of recommended measures requires actions by federal authorities. However, state authorities of the RB and Irkutsk Oblast also should take an active part in implementing the measures outlined in Table 7.2.

Table 7.2. **"Implementability" and estimated period of implementation**

Measure	"Implementability"	Period of implementation	
		Based on the scope of work	Taking into account political, social and economic acceptability
Establishment of State Corporation "The Fund for Support to the Baikal Natural Area", and provision of legislative, organisational and financial support	Low	1-2 years (first stage); 3-4 years (all authorised activity)	1-2 years (first stage); 3-4 years (all authorised activity)
Assigning the SC with responsibility for development of a system of support to the water sector of soft loans extended on a competitive basis		2-3 years	2-3 years

Source: Authors' recommendations and estimates.

The interrelated measures shall be implemented in the order as recommended above.

Expected outcome

- enhanced efficiency and cost-effectiveness of state support to the water sector and improved performance of state budget regarding sustainable development of the BNA and the RB, in general, via the establishment of the State Corporation "The Fund for Support to the Baikal Natural Area"
- assignment to SC of developing a system of support to the water sector, foremost through soft loans extended on a competitive basis
- increased rates of growth of GRP in RB, and of revenue of the consolidated budget of the RB and RF.

7.3. Facilitation of, and support to, implementation of wastewater treatment technologies to enable the attainment of standards for quality of water objects located within the BNA

Problem description

At present, some WSS companies in the RB discharge wastewater into water objects without permits. They can do this because draft standards for allowable discharges of substances and microorganisms, designed by these same companies, have not been approved in the established order. This happened because treatment facilities fail to meet sanitary standards and regulations for treatment of wastewater while the companies lack funds to modernise the facilities (for more detail, see Report #1 and sub-section 2.4.1 of this report).

Outline of measures

1. Develop a package of standard technical solutions to enable the achievement of wastewater treatment standards and guidelines for their implementation.

With such a package on hand, water users, not least WSS companies could reduce costs associated with the development of relevant projects on improving wastewater treatment.

2. Implement a package of projects in the RB to ensure that wastewater discharged into water objects eventually meets water quality standards. To that end, the following measures are recommended:

- Approve procedure for co-financing projects for upgrading of wastewater treatment stations by state authorities of the RF.
- Design and realise projects for upgrading of wastewater treatment stations.

Some important measures, specifically in Ulan-Ude, were included into the FTP "Protection of Lake Baikal and Socio-Economic Development of the Baikal Natural Area". In general, the main obstacle for implementation of measures is a lack of required funds. The measures may be financed by any public budget (municipal/regional/federal). Participation of a dedicated fund for support to the BNA in financing of the projects is also possible (see sub-section 2.5.2).

Estimated incremental cost and fiscal effect

The cost of the relevant work is estimated at RUB 1 000-1 500 million (based on expert estimates that consider the cost of comparable facilities in the RF).

Implementing the measures: level of authority and relationship with the Russian Federation's water policy

Regional authorities are able to carry out measures (Table 7.3) with support from federal funds and a dedicated fund for support to the BNA (provided that such fund is established). The recommended measures may be carried out independently of one another.

Table 7.3. **"Implementability" and estimated period of implementation**

Measure	"Implementability"	Period of implementation	
		Based on the scope of work	Taking into account political, social and economic acceptability
Developing a package of standard technical solutions to achieve wastewater treatment standards, and guidelines for their implementation	Moderate	1-2 years	1-2 years
Implementing a package of projects in the RB to ensure that wastewater discharged into water objects eventually meets water quality standards	Moderate	3-4 years	5-7 years

Source: Authors' recommendations and estimates.

Expected outcome

- compliance of wastewater discharged into water objects with the requirements of the RF legislation, reduction in discharges of polluting substances into Lake Baikal basin.

7.4. Supporting the development of storm water collector drainage systems, local water disposal systems, reduction and clean-up of discharges of liquid domestic waste into Lake Baikal

Problem description

Centralised storm water collector drainage systems are designed for in-take of rain water, snowmelt water, infiltration water, road washings and drainage water. Across the RB, these systems are available only in the city of Ulan-Ude where the system covers only 2.8% of the total length of the city's street and road network. Since the system cannot handle the actual volumes of wastewater, storm water is discharged into the Selenga River untreated.

Federal law "On General Principals of Organisation of Local Self-Governance in the Russian Federation" (#131-FZ, 6 October 2003) assigns responsibility for managing wastewater disposal, including by means of centralised storm water collector drainage systems, to local governments. Federal regulations oblige use of a storm water collector drainage system to help protect territories from floods and ground water flooding.[6] However, the city of Ulan-Ude does not have funds to meet this requirement, like most municipalities in the RF.

A significant factor contributing to pollution of water resources of Lake Baikal is that individual wastewater is disposed in coastal areas and rivers flowing into Lake Baikal within the territory of the RB. Additionally, some areas suffer from discharges of liquid domestic waste into Lake Baikal. The RF Water Code prohibits discharges of wastewater, and drainage water into water objects that contain natural therapeutic resources and that are included on a list of specially protected water objects. In that regard, the RF Code of Administrative Offences envisages penalties for violation of regulations on discharge of wastewater into water objects. In practice, however, administrative enforcement measures appear to be ineffective. Economic incentives must be introduced to solve the problem.

Outline of measures

1. Promote development of storm water collector drainage systems in Ulan-Ude in the following ways:

- Envisage (by local governments) rehabilitation and development of storm water collector drainage systems and inclusion of relevant works on a list of water supply and sanitation measures.
- Develop, approve and implement a Programme for Development of Storm Water Collector Drainage Systems in Ulan-Ude with financial support from the proposed SC "The Fund for Support to the Baikal Natural Area" (see sub-section 2.5.2).

2. Develop individual (on-site) sanitation, as well as liquid domestic waste and wastewater disposal facilities in coastal areas and rivers flowing into Lake Baikal:

- Elaborate and approve (by state authorities of the RB) wastewater disposal and centralised treatment of wastewater and liquid domestic waste in the BNA.
- Develop, approve and implement a regional programme for the rehabilitation and construction of systems of centralised treatment of wastewater and liquid domestic waste in the BNA with financial support from the SC "The Fund for Support to the Baikal Natural Area".

3. Prohibit the use of cesspools and septic tanks, in the BNA, if they are not equipped with individual (on-site) wastewater treatment facility.

The above measure implies amending federal laws and establishing an obligatory transitional period (at least 3-5 years). Another essential aspect envisages the approval of a procedure for providing targeted assistance to low-income households obliged to have toilets with septic tanks equipped with individual (on-site) wastewater treatment systems. The assistance could be financed from the regional budget and a dedicated fund (provided this is established).

Estimated incremental cost and fiscal effect

The cost of Measure 1 is about RUB 1 billion. Note that estimates in a 1990 feasibility study of Ulan-Ude engineering flood protection were RUB 17 billion (in 2012 prices) to build storm water collector drainage infrastructure and treatment facilities. That estimate reflected complicated relief, severe winters, seismic safety requirements, length of networks and so on. Measure 2 is estimated at RUB 500 million; Measure 3 would cost about RUB 500 million (based on expert estimates that consider the cost of comparable facilities in the RF).

Considering the substantial amount of finance required, the practicability of the measure appears to be low in the short run.

Implementing the measures: level of authority and relationship with the Russian Federation's water policy

Regional authorities are able to implement Measures 1-2 (see Table 7.4) with financial support from the federal budget and a dedicated fund for support to the BNA, provided such a fund is established. Implementation of Measure 3 requires actions by federal authorities as it relates to amending federal legislation; while regional authorities should implement what relates to the RB. All measures aim to improve efficiency of WRM in the BNA and may be carried out independently of one another.

Table 7.4. **"Implementability" and estimated period of implementation**

Measure	"Implementability"	Period of implementation	
		Based on the scope of work	Taking into account political, social and economic acceptability
Promoting the development of storm water collector drainage systems in Ulan-Ude	Low	3-4 years	3-4 years
Improving individual (on-site) wastewater treatment and disposal systems in coastal areas and along rivers flowing into Lake Baikal	Low	3-4 years	3-4 years
Prohibiting the use of cesspools and septic tanks, in the BNA, if they are not equipped with individual (on-site) wastewater treatment facility	Low	3-5 years	5-7 years

Source: Authors' recommendations and estimates.

Expected outcome

- improved environmental situation in the RB's water sector, better prevention of flooding of municipal territories caused by storm water
- better prevention of pollution of rivers and water resources relating to Lake Baikal basin from storm water and wastewater from cesspools and septic tanks.

Notes

1. For more details, see Section 5 in Report #1 and Section 6 in Report #2.
2. See, for example, Zhigalov D.V. and Pertzov L.V (2011).
3. In the near future, federal legislation may provide for setting a resort fee. Nevertheless, the redistribution of the relevant revenue between municipalities located in the BNA and the SC requires special legal provisions.
4. If ecosystem services are provided by private entities using private resources, all proceeds should of course be their own revenues; but if ecosystem services are provided by publicly-owned ecosystems or by public entities, all or part of respective proceeds could well (and should be) appropriated to the public budget, or to the proposed SC.
5. It is advisable that the relevant experience of Austria, reviewed in Section 6 of Report #2, be used.
6. See Federal Law "Technical Regulations on Safety of Buildings and Facilities" (#384-ФЗ, 30.12.2009), and the RF Government Decree "Technical Protection of Territories, Buildings, and Facilities from Hazardous Geological Processes. General Provisions" (#1047-p, 21.06.2010, SNiP 22 February 2003).

References

Federal Law "Technical Regulations on Safety of Buildings and Facilities" (#384-ФЗ, 30.12.2009).

Federal Law "On Non-Profit Organisations" (#7-ФЗ, dated 12 January 1996).

Federal law "On general principals of organisation of local self-governance in the Russian Federation".

Government of the Russian Federation, Decree "Technical Protection of Territories, Buildings, and Facilities from Hazardous Geological Processes. General Provisions" (#1047-p, 21.06.2010, SNiP 22 February 2003).

Government of the Russian Federation, Decree "On Federal Target Programme "Protection of Lake Baikal and Socio-Economic Development of the Baikal Natural Area in 2012-2020" (21 August 2012, #847).

Zhigalov D.V. and Pertzov L.V (2011), "*Financial Principles of Local Self-Governance: Outcomes of the 2000ies*" // Budget, #7, 2011.

Chapter 8

Instruments for better managing risks associated with water resources in Buryatia

In the context of water resources, the most acute problem facing Buryatia consists in ineffective management of risks arising from water-related hazards. To address the problem, this chapter recommends:

(i) delineation of the Baikal Natural area (BNA) into Red, Yellow, and Green zones according to the probability of water-related emergency events, and the size of potential damage; and

(ii) application of specific risk management instruments in each zone, including:

– strengthening supervision for compliance with the ban on new civil construction projects within the territories exposed to extremely high risks of water-related hazards (Red zone);

– promotion of compulsory insurance against the risk of water-related hazards in the Yellow zone;

– differentiation of land tax and property tax rates with due account for availability of infrastructure for protection from water-related hazards; and

– introduction of compulsory insurance against non-critical risks for water resources and ecosystems in the BNA.

Recent mud-flow due to collapse of an alpine lake in Buryatia highlighted ineffectiveness of management of risks arising from water-related hazards.

As described at previous stages of the project (see Reports #1 and #2), the risks associated with water resources may fall into two main groups: environmental risks to water resources and the related ecosystems and biodiversity, and the risks of water-related hazards such as wind setups, mud flows, floods, ground water flooding, etc.

The system of management of the above risks is designed to provide the safety of both water resources and of the population living close to water objects. Establishing a risk management system implies, at a minimum, the development of mechanisms for monitoring, assessment, prevention, mitigation or minimisation of the risks, and minimisation of the associated damage. The system should provide for comprehensive and regular activity in respect of risk management, and promote incentives for reducing the probability of respective risk and minimising the ensuing damage.

In the context of water resources, the most acute problem facing the RB consists in ineffective management of risks arising from water-related hazards.

These recommendations on **managing risks of water-related hazards** suggest the development and implementation of a uniform classification of the RB's areas prone to water-related hazards, and graded in the following way, according to the probability (or likelihood) of water-related emergency events, and the size of possible damage:

- Red Zone – areas with extremely high and unacceptable risk of hazards, or unacceptable size of potential damage
- Yellow Zone – areas with high risk and considerable potential damage (but not a catastrophic one)
- Green Zone – areas with minor risk and minor potential damage.

This comprehensive approach envisages, among other things, improving the prevention system and minimising negative consequences of floods and mud flows. Determining what level of risk and potential damage should be considered as high, acceptable or unacceptable (catastrophic) is a political decision that should be part of a policy dialogue between stakeholders in the RB.

Specific instruments should be used to manage the risk of water-related hazards in respect of each of the outlined above zones.

Red Zone suggests the use of direct prohibitions and constraints to new construction projects and introduction of compulsory insurance for existing real estate and life insurance for people who work or live there (see section 8.1).

Yellow Zone is associated with compulsory insurance of existing real estate and other fixed assets, as well as life insurance for people who work or live there (see section 8.2).

In regard to **Green Zone** the foregoing prohibitions and rules do not apply, but voluntary life insurance and property insurance should be promoted.

The relevant international practice (see Report #2) and inadequate development of commercial insurance market in the RF support the conclusion that only public insurance against the risk of water-related hazards could be viable, and it should be provided. In addition, assessment of susceptibility of the RB's areas to water-related hazards should be considered when establishing higher rates of taxes for land and property in respect to land plots, real estate items and other economic assets located in Red and Yellow Zones (see section 8.3).

For **management of risks to water resources and related ecosystems and biodiversity**, it is recommended to introduce a system of compulsory liability insurance to strengthen the responsibility for liquidation of, and compensation for, the damage caused to the environment and third parties (see section 8.4).

8.1. Strengthening supervision for compliance with the ban on new civil construction projects within the territories exposed to extremely high risks of water-related hazards

Problem description

The RB typically has a high probability of occurrence of flooding, mud flows, icing, gullying and river wash, waterlogging and siltation of river beds. These factors create emergency situations and cause damage to the population and the economy of the republic. Most rivers have considerable flow rates (2.2-3.0 m/sec), steep drop and their narrow valleys predetermine dramatic water surges in the rainy seasons. Catastrophic floods submerge over 300 settlements in the RB, including 17 large settlements and farms, destruction of bridges, residential buildings, power and communication lines. They wash out roads, and lead to loss of fertile soil and soil sedimentation. According to the RB state programme "Environmental Protection and Sustainable Use of Natural Resources", 196 300 people, or about 20% of the total population, live in territories vulnerable to water-related hazards. As expected, the number of affected persons may be about 15% of the total population of the RB.

The most complex situation takes place in Ulan-Ude. Major damage from flood was registered in 1993, when the entire left-bank of the city was inundated. The zone of submergence encompassed more than 9 000 summer cottages, 8 250 buildings, 36 000 ha of farmland, 60 farms, 250 km of roads, 58 bridges, 1 800 km of communication lines and 2 800 km of power lines.

The RB Urban Planning Regulations provide for land-use planning and management procedures with consideration for a special regime of economic activities in the BNA in complex geotechnical, natural and climatic conditions. The RB's urban planning scheme determines, in particular, zones with special-use conditions, and boundaries of territories prone to risk of emergencies caused by natural and human-made disasters. It also envisages constraints in regard to construction in zones of flooding and catastrophic inundation, and identifies land zoning.

Supervision for compliance with the ban on implementation of new construction projects within the territories prone to flooding should take place at the stage of developing and implementing both land-use and urban planning. Although implementation of the new construction projects is prohibited on the territories prone to flooding, **the ban appears to be violated on a large scale.**

Outline of measures

1. Strengthen responsibility for violation of the ban on new construction projects within the territories exposed to the extremely high risk of water-related hazards. Implementation requires changes in the RF Code of Administrative Offences and, if required, other regulatory legal acts.

2. Conduct public awareness campaigns and regular awareness work among the population and legal entities about the risk of water-related hazards. These measures involve spreading information (via mass media) about frequently inundated territories that

tend to be dangerous for living and economic activities, and about the level of potential risks and the size of possible associated damage.

Estimated incremental cost and fiscal effect

Measures could be implemented as part of the routine work of public authorities at zero direct incremental cost. Direct influence on budget revenue also appears to be non-existent. Assessment of the relevant results and fiscal effect requires special research and analysis, although these are beyond the scope of the present project.

Implementing the measures: level of authority and relationship with the Russian Federation's water policy

The outlined measures (Table 8.1) are a component of water policy in the RF. Federal authorities should implement measures to strengthen responsibility for failure to comply with the ban on implementation of new construction projects within the territories exposed to extremely high risk of water-related hazards. The bodies of state power of the RB have power to implement measures to strengthen supervision for compliance with the ban on implementation of new construction projects within the territories prone to mud flows, flooding and ground water submergence, within the boundaries of the BNA in the RB.

Table 8.1. **"Implementability" and estimated period of implementation**

Measure	"Implementability"	Period of implementation	
		Based on the scope of work	Taking into account political, social and economic acceptability
Strengthening responsibility for violation of the ban on new construction projects within the territories exposed to extremely high risk of water-related hazards	Moderate	1-3 years	1-3 years
Conducting public awareness campaigns about the risk of water-related hazards among population and legal entities	High	1-2 years	1-2 years

Source: Authors' recommendations and estimates.

The recommended measures may be carried out independently of one another.

Expected outcome

- fewer violations of the ban on new construction projects within the territories prone to water-related hazards, and more revenue to the budget if violation of the ban persists
- more awareness of population and economic entities in regard to boundaries of the territories prone to high risk of flooding and fewer economic losses from water-related hazards.

8.2. Promotion of system of compulsory insurance against the risk of water-related hazards in the BNA[1]

Problem description

Insurance is an essential component and key economic instrument for managing the risk of water-related hazards. Even with low probability of risk, an incident may entail very serious implications and damage.

International practice suggests, however, that commercial insurance against the risk of a natural disaster is complex, and requires considerable finance. The system of insurance against the above-mentioned risks also tends to be undermined by well-known problems of "moral hazard" and "adverse selection" (attractive for persons with the highest risks, and not attractive for applicants least prone and vulnerable to risk because of unreasonably high insurance premiums). Since the risks cannot be spread out geographically, the loss modelling and assessment of adequate amount of insurance premium (that is, the instruments for conventional insurance) are still limited.

All that said, as follows from relevant international practice, the introduction of compulsory insurance for non-critical risks of water-related hazards may enhance, drastically, the efficiency of risk management in the BNA.

In connection with the above-mentioned "market failures", the insurance against the risk of water-related hazards tends to be in the hands of the public rather than private sector. And the state establishes base rates that could vary, additionally, according to an insurance agent. In cases where immovable propriety is at high risk of mud flows and floods, compliance with requirements to reduce risk is considerably costly to owners. This discourages new construction projects in the high-risk zone.

Introduction of compulsory insurance against the risk of water-related hazards should rely on statistical analysis of floods and mud flows. Specifically, the system should take into account different probabilities of water-related hazards. It should also consider performance of the insured party as it relates to mitigating the risk of water-related hazards and potential damage if the risk materialises, and encourage preventive measures. This corresponds to international practice and should be considered in the RB provided it introduces an insurance system following the recommendations.

Outline of measures

1. Amend the federal law on environmental protection, including provisions for a pilot system of compulsory insurance against the risk of water-related hazards in the BNA. The insurance should cover risks to life and health of individuals who live or work in high-risk areas, and the risks to immovable property and stocks of commodities and materials located in the above-mentioned areas. Federal regulations should also be changed as needed.

The insurance system should be adjusted in accordance with a scheme of state compensation for damage to property of population caused by water-related hazards. According to Report #1, it is impossible to entirely abandon use of compensation schemes. On the negative side, the scheme fails to rely on "colour signals" for people who live in danger zones, and entails considerable costs and losses. An improved system should create incentives for insured persons to undertake preventive measures taking into account different probabilities of insured risks on different territories, and also address the moral hazard problem effectively. With this in mind, we also recommend applying some instruments that give such signals (for example, increased land tax rates and property tax rates in respect of territories prone to high risks of water-related hazards) (see sub-section 2.6.3).

In the long run, possible mechanisms might consider the premium applied for public insurance of properties, land tax rates and property tax rates. This would lead immediately to incremental rates and serve as a signal to owners. The mechanism is a good example of how to replicate the international practice of comprehensive economic instruments for WRM. Implementation of this promising instrument, however, would be possible only after comprehensive changes to federal tax legislation.

Losses should be divided between the insurer (the state) and the insured party to encourage economic agents to carefully assess and consider the risks of living or purchasing fixed assets in areas of high risk of water-related hazards.

2. Introduce a comprehensive pilot system of compulsory insurance against the risk of water-related hazards in the BNA. This involves carrying out the measures below:

- Elaborate a technique for determining and assessing the risk of water-related hazards, and monitoring procedures (including a targeted set of incentives).
- Provide legislative and organisational support to introduce a system of compulsory insurance against the risk of water-related hazards in the BNA, including monitoring, assessment and minimisation of risks and related losses through preventive measures.

Estimated incremental cost and fiscal effect

Relevant estimates require special research and analysis that are beyond the scope of the project. As might be expected, however, one-off expenses for implementing the system (including expenses for training staff), would save, in the long run, a substantial amount of budget funds to be used for compensation of damage from water-related hazards. The payments would cover clean-up of the aftermath of natural disasters in high-risk areas and compensation to the affected party.

Implementing the measures: level of authority involved and relationship with the Russian Federation's water policy

The measures aim at improving the efficiency of WRM in the BNA. Federal authorities have sufficient power to implement the first stage of measures outlined in Table 8.2 while regional authorities are able to follow up with implementation of pilot projects. If the measures prove successful, other regions of the RF could replicate the practice provided that relevant decisions are made at the federal level.

Table 8.2. **"Implementability" and estimated period of implementation**

		Period of implementation	
Measure	**"Implementability"**	**Based on the scope of work**	**Taking into account political, social and economic acceptability**
Amending federal laws on environmental protection, and including provisions on creation of a pilot system of compulsory insurance against the risks of water-related hazards in the BNA	Moderate	2-3 years	2-3 years
Introducing a comprehensive pilot system of compulsory insurance of the risks of water-related hazards in the BNA, including monitoring, assessment and minimisation of the risks and of related losses		3-5 years	3-5 years

Source: Authors' recommendations and estimates.

The interrelated measures shall be implemented as presented above.

Expected outcome

- a pilot system of insurance against the risk of water-related hazards in the BNA and dissemination of the relevant practice in other regions of the RF if the measure proves to be a success
- mitigation or minimisation of economic and social damage caused by water-related hazards
- saving of public funds to be invested in cleaning up after natural disasters in high-risk areas and used for compensation payments to the affected party.

8.3. Differentiation of land tax rates and property tax rates with due account for availability and quality of infrastructure for protection from water-related hazards

Problem description

As mentioned above, the supervision for compliance with the ban on new construction projects within the territories prone to flooding and mud flows appears to be inadequate within the RB. In the region, however, as all over the world, the price of land plots in such areas generally tends to be lower, making them more attractive for new construction projects; at the same time, economic interest for new construction projects in such areas appears to be higher. With public insurance in place, this issue gives rise to the risk of an unreasonably heavy load on the budget for compensating losses suffered by insured parties.

In the RF, land tax falls under municipal jurisdiction, which means that local governments set land tax rates within the range of 0.3-1.5% of the cadastral value of a land plot, as approved by the RF Tax Code. The relevant tax revenue goes to municipal budgets.

The established tax rate multiplied by the cadastral value of the respective land plot determines the amount of land tax payable. A cadastral value is determined by appraiser companies based on their own techniques, and should be revised at least once every five years. At present, land tax rates typically do not consider the risk of mud flows and floods, and, by no means, discourage civil construction in areas prone to water-related hazards. The same occurs in respect of property (real estate) tax. Regional bodies of state power and local governments share responsibility for the relevant decisions regarding property of legal entities and property of individuals, respectively.

Outline of measures

International practice shows that use of the land tax and property tax (as it relates to immovable property) could help create incentives and disincentives for construction of new buildings and facilities in areas of high risk of water-related hazards. With this in view, the following measures could be carried out to encourage local governments to establish incremental rates of land tax and property tax (as it relates to immovable property) in respect of the areas prone to water-related hazards (mud flows, floods, landslides, etc.).

1. Develop and approve (by regional bodies of state power of the RB) the procedural framework for differentiation of land tax and property tax with due account for:

- classification of territories in the RB prone to water-related hazards according to the degree of probability that they will experience emergencies associated with water, as well as the size of potential or expected damage
- procedure for calculating incremental rates of land tax and property tax (as it relates to immovable property) in respect of areas prone to water-related hazards

(estimate of probability should consider availability and quality of infrastructure for protection from the above-mentioned emergencies) and potential ensuing damage.

In regard to land tax and individual property tax, the above-mentioned guidelines should be approved by a decree of the RB government. The decree should also envisage recommendations to local governments of the RB on setting higher rates in respect of the territories prone to mud flows and floods. Regional legislation should provide additional guidelines on corporate property tax.

2. Assign local governments the right to establish incremental rates of land tax and individual property tax in respect of the areas prone to water-related hazards, and amend the RB Tax Code accordingly.

The provision should be deemed reasonable because many municipalities have already established maximum rates of land tax and individual property tax in respect to all tax payers; further increase of rates appears to be impossible within the existing legal and regulatory framework.

Estimated incremental cost and fiscal effect

The cost of research is estimated at RUB 10-20 million (major costs are related to evaluating the degree of susceptibility of the area to emergencies, and to training for staff of local self-governance bodies). On the whole, increased revenues from land tax to the RB due to use of special factors is estimated at 20% of the present level, or RUB 90-100 million per year (in 2014 prices).

Implementing the measures: level of authority and relationship with Russian Federation's water policy

Implementation of the recommended measures (Table 8.3) requires actions by bodies of state power of the RB in the first place; while federal bodies of state power should implement measures relating to setting of incremental factors (as a common element of RF water policy). Responsibility for establishing incremental tax rates should be assigned to local governments (in respect of land tax and individual property tax) and regional bodies of state power of the RB (in respect of corporate property tax).

Table 8.3. **"Implementability" and estimated period of implementation**

		Period of implementation	
Measure	"Implementability"	Based on the scope of work	Taking into account political, social and economic acceptability
Developing and approving (by regional bodies of state power of the RB) the procedural framework for differentiation of land tax and property tax	Moderate	1-2 years	1-2 years
Assigning local governments the right to establish incremental rates of land tax and individual property tax in respect of the areas prone to water-related hazards; and amending the RB Tax Code accordingly	Low	6 months-1 year	6 months-1 year

Source: Authors' recommendations and estimates.

Recommended measures may be carried out independently.

Expected outcome

- creation of economic incentives for drastically reducing the volumes of civil construction in areas prone to floods and other forms of water-related hazards against the backdrop of slumping demand for land plots, buildings, facilities and residential premises in the above areas.

8.4. Introduction of system of compulsory insurance against non-critical risks for water resources, related ecosystems and biodiversity in the BNA

Problem description

Introducing a system of compulsory insurance against non-critical risks for water resources, related ecosystems and biodiversity in the BNA (against non-critical environmental risks, in a broader sense) appears to be an important measure. It would reflect the logic of recommendations to partially replace administrative mechanisms with market mechanisms (to the extent possible given the potential impact on the unique ecosystem of the BNA).

As already noted above, international practice of insurance against environmental risks looks rather patchy. It provides quite a few examples of "market failures" associated with commercial insurance against above risks. In view of the practice and unsustainable market of commercial insurance against environmental risks, either public insurance or a blend of public and private insurance are the feasible forms of insurance to date.

The system of compulsory insurance against environmental risks for water resources and related ecosystems and biodiversity should be streamlined in accordance with the changes (mitigation) of administrative bans in respect of selected types of economic activities in the BNA. In this way, insurance will only be provided to those activities that do not entail any tremendous "irreversible" damage to the ecosystem, even as a result of the most unfavourable development of events. Special research is needed to identify all activities for which the existing ban can be lifted and replaced by obligatory insurance, and a list of such activities should be prepared.

Outline of measures

1. Amend federal laws on environmental protection. Provisions should include creation of a pilot system of compulsory insurance against non-critical environmental risks and the ensuing responsibility for clean-up and compensation for damage and losses caused to the environment and third parties. Respective federal bylaws might be amended accordingly, as needed.

2. Introduce, in the BNA, a comprehensive pilot system of compulsory insurance of non-critical environmental risks and liability for clean-up and compensation for damage and losses caused to the environment and third parties through the following:

- Develop a technique for determining and assessing non-critical environmental risk, and the related monitoring methods.
- Provide legislative and organisational support to introduce a system of compulsory insurance against non-critical risk for water resources and the related ecosystems and biodiversity in the BNA.

Implementation of the measure requires a long transition (5-10 years) and consideration for relevant international practice. Qualified insurance agents should also be selected among reliable banks and insurance companies.

Estimated incremental cost and fiscal effect

Estimate of the cost and effects of the measures requires special research and analysis. These, however, are beyond the scope of the project.

Implementing the measures: level of authority and relationship with the Russian Federation's water policy

The measures (Table 8.4) seek to improve the efficiency of WRM in the BNA. Federal authorities are able implement the first stage of activities, while regional authorities should follow-up with implementation of a pilot project. If the measures prove successful, other regions of the RF might replicate the practice provided that relevant decisions are made at the federal level.

Table 8.4. **"Implementability" and estimated period of implementation**

Measure	"Implementability"	Period of implementation	
		Based on the scope of work	Taking into account political, social and economic acceptability
Amending federal laws on environmental protection to include provisions on creation of a pilot system of compulsory insurance against non-critical environmental risks and the ensuing responsibility for clean-up and compensation for damage and losses caused to the environment and third parties	Moderate	2-3 years	2-3 years
Introducing, in the BNA, a comprehensive pilot system of compulsory insurance of non-critical environmental risks and liability for clean-up and compensation for damage and losses caused to the environment and third parties		4-5 years	5-10 years

Source: Authors' recommendations and estimates.

The interrelated measures shall be implemented in the order recommended above.

Expected outcome

- a pilot system of compulsory insurance against environmental risks introduced in the BNA, and relevant practice disseminated in other regions of the Russian Federation if the pilot measure proves to be a success
- reduced socio-economic losses from environmental degradation and of the amount of public budget funds spent for clean-up of consequences of water-related hazards and compensation for damage and losses.

Note

1. Within the limits of "Yellow zone" as described above.

Chapter 9

Factors essential for implementing the recommendations

This chapter discusses factors essential for implementation of the recommendations (legislative, economic and financial; information and knowledge gaps) and offers some proposals on how to manage the implementation process.

Factors essential for implementing the recommendations

Factors essential for implementing the recommendations

For implementation of the recommendations on improving economic instruments for water resources management (WRM) in Buryatia outlined in Part II of this report, the following factors would be essential:

- "Political will" and good co-operation: between the levels of state governance system and with influential stakeholders with significant lobbying capabilities (e.g. energy sector), as well as environmental and civil society organisations.
- Legislative: The centralised legal regulation in Russia means that many federal legal acts must be amended before the recommended measures can be implemented.
- Economic and financial: the RB's authorities cannot provide for full-scale maintenance and rehabilitation of water infrastructure without financial support from the RF.
- Mismatch between the boundaries of the RB and the BNA.
- Information and knowledge gaps: information for decision-making and control in regard to the ecosystem of Lake Baikal is scarce; special scientific research should be conducted before implementing some of the recommendations.

They are discussed in more detail below:

Mismatch between the boundaries of the RB and the BNA. The present administrative-territorial division is characterised by a mismatch between the boundaries of the Republic of Buryatia (RB) and the Baikal Natural Area (BNA). Lake Baikal basin encompasses 52% of the territory of the RB. The rest of the basin's territory belongs to the Yenisei River and Lena River basins. At the same time, 57.1% of the BNA lies within the boundaries of the RB, and the watercourses formed in its territory has a decisive influence on the state of water resources and the ecosystem of Lake Baikal. In some cases, this fact complicates recommendations since they require joint participation of the bodies of state power of the RB and Irkutsk Oblast. Such cases should be specified separately. A third region, *Zabaikalski Krai*, also contributes to the BNA territory, although it influences the ecosystem of Lake Baikal to a lesser extent than the RB and Irkutsk Oblast.

On the positive side, the above mismatch increases the importance of the RB as a testing ground for pilot solutions that might be replicated at the federal level later on. Since most WRM in the BNA will take place in the RB, individual solutions are needed for the BNA with its unique water resources, and for the territories relating to other basin areas. Technically, this would enable tailor-made and, therefore, more adaptive solutions in terms of their further replication.

Institutional factors

"Political will" and good co-operation between the levels of state governance: With a strongly centralised governance system in the RF, decision-making in regard to the most important issues of governance is in the domain of federal authorities in the Russian Federation. In addition, the BNA-related goal setting differs when undertaken by federal authorities and the RB's regional authorities. Federal authorities want to protect Lake Baikal and the BNA from the negative impact of man-made, production-induced and natural factors. Regional authorities, however, have to strike a balance between protecting Lake Baikal and the BNA from negative effects and promoting sustainable economic development of the region.

Influential stakeholders: Co-operation with industries, environmental and civil society organisations is key. But the structure of the RB's economy discourages the arrival of large companies with substantial capabilities and resources to influence federal decision-making. While operators of the Angara HES cascade in Irkutsk Oblast (OAO "*RusHydro*", OAO "*Irkutsk Energo*") and some major consumers of electricity (e.g. aluminium producers) have huge lobbying capacities in regard to federal decision-making.

Legislative factors: Legal regulation is centralised in the RF. The recommendations, roughly, fall into three groups:

- measures focusing on the water sector of the RF, at large, (including the water sector in the RB), with federal authorities being responsible for implementing thereof;
- measures assigned to bodies of state power of the RB (regional authorities) that concern the BNA, but could be carried out only after the creation of enabling legislative environment by bodies of state power of the RF (federal authorities)
- measures that could be implemented by regional authorities within the existing regulatory legal framework.

The second group of recommendations is the largest. The third group is the smallest; due to centralisation of the regulatory system, few measures could be implemented without amending the federal acts. This requires good political will and co-operation between the levels of state governance system.

Economic and financial factors: Economic development of the RB tends to be below the national average; the regional economy lacks enterprises of national importance and top enterprises are subsidiaries of large holding companies managed from outside the RB. As a result, the region's financial and budgetary system relies heavily on federal transfers; the RB's authorities cannot provide for a full-scale maintenance and rehabilitation of water infrastructure in the absence of financial support from the RF.

Key stakeholders: The structure of the RB's economy discourages the arrival of large companies with substantial capabilities and resources to influence federal decision-making. While operators of the Angara HES cascade in Irkutsk Oblast (OAO "RusHydro", OAO "Irkutsk Energo") and some major consumers of electricity (e.g. aluminium producers) have huge lobbying capacities in regard to federal decision-making.

Information and knowledge gaps

Comprehensive information about the ecosystem of Lake Baikal for decision-making is absent. On the one hand, the existing system of environmental monitoring fails to provide complete information about the status of water objects in the BNA on a regular basis. On the other, the RF's system of governance, as distinct from most member states of the EU and the OECD, has no experience in using many economic instruments for WRM. With that in mind, implementation of many recommendations requires special research both in relation to the impact assessment on the ecosystem of the BNA and to effective and economic solutions, as well as the legal framework allowing for their implementation. The required research is described in the recommendations and summarised in Annex B.

Proposals on how to manage the implementation process

With the aim of improving instruments for WRM of Lake Baikal in the RB, an extensive set of considerably interrelated measures has been suggested. For the most part, these require active participation of federal authorities. In that regard, **a special plan of measures on implementing and streamlining the instruments for water management in the RB (an Action Plan)** might be elaborated and approved.

The recommendations might provide a foundation for the above plan after discussions with concerned ministries and agencies, NGOs and environmental organisations. The recommendations might also be refined with due consideration of proposals and comments from federal level stakeholders. Refining the plan of measures might take place with participation of a special task group established under the auspices of the Inter-Agency Commission for Conservation of Lake Baikal. In the authors' opinion, responsibility for supervising the development of the plan of measures should be assigned to a representative of the RF government holding an office of a deputy prime minister. The elaborated and adjusted plan of measures (Action Plan) should be approved by a decree of the RF government.

It would require a huge amount of inter-agency work to implement the Action Plan. In this connection, the established special task force should work on a regular basis during the implementation period. Staff of respective public authorities needs to be trained on how to implement the proposed recommendations. In addition, a special system to monitor progress of implementation and for introduction and streamlining of instruments for WRM in the RB should be set up.

Annex A

Bibliography of the project

This Annex lists all legal acts and publications that informed the project and the Interim and Final Reports 1, 2 and 3.

Federal legal and regulatory acts [1]

Government of the Russian Federation, Budget Code (31 July 1998, #145-ФЗ).

Government of the Russian Federation, Tax Code, Part One (31 July 1998, #146-ФЗ) and Part Two (5 August 2000, #117-ФЗ).

Government of the Russian Federation, Land Code (25 October 2001,#136-ФЗ).

Government of the Russian Federation, Code of Administrative Offences (30 December 2001, #195-ФЗ).

Government of the Russian Federation, Housing Code (29 December 2004,#188-ФЗ).

Government of the Russian Federation, Water Code (3 June 2006, #74-ФЗ).

Government of the Russian Federation, Forestry Code (4 December 2006, #200-ФЗ).

Government of the Russian Federation, Federal Law "On Sub-soil Resources' (21 February 1992, #2395-1).

Government of the Russian Federation, Federal Law "On Specially Protected Natural Areas" (14 March 1995, #33-ФЗ).

Government of the Russian Federation, Federal Law "On Environmental Impact Assessment" (23 November 1995, #174-ФЗ).

Government of the Russian Federation, Federal Law "On Non-Profit Organisations" (12 January 1996, #7-ФЗ).

Government of the Russian Federation, Federal Law "On Protection of Lake Baikal" (1 May 1999, #94-ФЗ).

Government of the Russian Federation, Federal Law "On Protection of Environment" (10 January 2002, #7-ФЗ).

Government of the Russian Federation, Federal Law "On General Principals of Organisation of Local Governance in the Russian Federation" (6 October 2003, #131-ФЗ).

Government of the Russian Federation, Federal Law "On General Principals of Tariff Setting for Utility Enterprises" (30 December 2004, #210-ФЗ).

Government of the Russian Federation, Federal Law "On Special Economic Zones" (22 July 2005, #116-ФЗ).

Government of the Russian Federation, Federal Law "Technical Regulations on Security of Buildings and Facilities" (30 December 2009, #384-ФЗ).

Government of the Russian Federation, Federal Law "On Water Supply and Sanitation" (7 December 2011, #416-ФЗ).

Government of the Russian Federation, Decree "On Environmental Land Use Planning of the Baikal Natural Area (BNA) and Provision of Information to Population about the Boundaries of the BNA, the Environmental Zones and the Relevant Regimes" (6 September 2000, #661).

Government of the Russian Federation, Decree "On the Acceptable Minimum Level of Water for Economic Activities and Other Types of Activities" (26 March 2001, #234).

Government of the Russian Federation, Decree "On Approving the List of Activities Prohibited in Central Environmental Zone of the BNA" (30 August 2001, #643).

Government of the Russian Federation, Decree "On Federal Target Programme "Ecology and Natural Resources of Russia" for 2002-2010" (7 December 2001, #860).

Government of the Russian Federation, Decree "On Specificity of Conservation, Capture Fisheries of Endemic Species of Shellfish and Gathering of Aquatic Plants in Lake Baikal" (28 January 2002, #67).

Government of the Russian Federation, Decree "Rates of Charges for Emission into the Atmosphere of Polluting Substances by Stationary and Mobile Sources of Pollution, Discharges of Polluting Substances into Surface and Underground Water Objects, Particularly from Centralised Sanitation Systems and Disposal of Production and Consumption Waste" (12 June 2003, #344).

Government of the Russian Federation, Decree "On Rates of Charges for the Use of Water Objects in Federal Ownership" (30 December 2006, #876).

Government of the Russian Federation, Decree "On Approving the Regulation on State Monitoring of Water objects" (10 April 2007, #219).

Government of the Russian Federation, Decree "On Federal Programme "Zhilishche" (Housing) for 2011-2015" (17 December 2010, #1050).

Government of the Russian Federation, Decree "On Federal Target Programme "Pure Water" (22 December 2010, #1092).

Government of the Russian Federation, Decree "On Federal Target Programme "Development of Water Management System of the Russian Federation in 2012-2020" (19 April 2012, #350).

Government of the Russian Federation, Decree "On Federal Target Programme "Protection of Lake Baikal and Socio-Economic Development of the Baikal Natural Area in 2012-2020" (21 August 2012, #847).

Government of the Russian Federation, Decree "On Groups of Users of Facilities in regard to which the Standards for Allowable Discharges of Polluting Substances, Other Substances, and Microorganisms into Water Objects are Set" (18 March 2013, #230).

Government of the Russian Federation, Decree "On Approving the Regulations on Reduction in the Amount of Charges for Negative Impact on the Environment on a Condition that Wastewater Treatment Companies and Their Users Implement Environmental Measures (17 April 2013, #347).

Government of the Russian Federation, Decree "On the State of Environmental Monitoring and State Database of the Relevant Data" (9 August 2013, #681).

Government of the Russian Federation, Decree "On Federal Target Programme "Development of Land Improvement of Agricultural Land for 201-2020" (12 October 2013, #922).

Government of the Russian Federation, Decree "On Approving the State Programme "Protection of the Environment for 2012-2020" (15 April 2014, #326).

Government of the Russian Federation, Resolution "On Boundaries of the Baikal Natural Area" (27 November 2006, #1641-p).

Government of the Russian Federation, Resolution "On Approving the Federal Plan of Statistical Work" (6 May 2008).

Government of the Russian Federation, Resolution "On Water Strategy of the Russian Federation till 2020" (27 August 2009, #1235-p).

Government of the Russian Federation, Resolution "On Approving the Strategy of Socio-Economic Development of the Far East and Baikal Region till 2025" (28 December 2009, #2094-p).

Government of the Russian Federation, Resolution "On the List of National Standards and the Body of Rules" (21 June 2010, #1047-p).

Government of the Russian Federation, Resolution "On Approving the Strategy of Socio-Economic Development of Siberia till 2020" (5 July 2010 #1120-p).

Government of the Russian Federation, Ministry of Agriculture, Order "On Approval of the Procedure for Determining the Charges for Service/Performance of Work (as it relates to its basic activities) Provided by Federal State Budget-Funded Institution for Land Improvement, under the Jurisdiction of the Ministry of Agriculture of the RF, to Individuals and Legal Entities" (18 February 2013, #79).

Government of the Russian Federation, Ministry of Finance, Order "On Enactment of International Financial Reporting Standards (IFRS) and Explaining the Use of the IFRS in the Russian Federation" (25 November 2011, #160н).

Government of the Russian Federation, Ministry of Natural Resources and Environmental Protection, Order "On Approval of Methodological Guidelines on Elaboration of Standards of Allowable Impact on Water objects" (12 December 2007, #328).

Government of the Russian Federation, Ministry of Natural Resources and Environmental Protection, Order "On Approval of Methodological Guidelines for Users of Water on Elaboration of Standards of Allowable Discharges of Substances and Microorganisms into Water objects" (17 December 2007, #333).

Government of the Russian Federation, Ministry of Natural Resources and Environmental Protection, Order "On Approval of Standards of the Maximum Allowable Impact on the Unique Ecosystem of Lake Baikal, and a List of Hazardous Substances, Particularly Extremely Hazardous Substances, Highly Hazardous Substances, Hazardous Substances, and Moderately Hazardous for the Unique Ecosystem of Lake Baikal" (5 March 2010, #63).

Government of the Russian Federation, Ministry of Regional Development, Order "On Approving the Methodological Guidelines on Calculation of the Maximum Growth Indices Utility Tariff Rates for Households" (23 August 2010, 378).

Legal and regulatory acts of the Republic of Buryatia

Republic of Buryatia, Law "On Selected Issues of Tax Regulation in the RB Assigned to Subjects of the RF by Federal (RF) Law on Taxes and Levies" (26 November 2002, #145-III).

Republic of Buryatia, Law "On the Budgeting Process in the Republic of Buryatia" (3 July 2007, #2359-III).

Republic of Buryatia, Law "On Strategy of Socio-Economic Development of the Republic of Buryatia till 2025" (15 December 2007, #410).

Republic of Buryatia, Law "On State Support of Investment Activities in the Republic of Buryatia" (8 May 2009, #868-IV).

Republic of Buryatia, Law "On the Programme of Socio-Economic Development of the Republic of Buryatia till 2020" (14 March 2011, #1903-IV).

Republic of Buryatia, Law "On the Programme of Socio-Economic Development of the Republic of Buryatia for 2011-2015" (14 March 2011, #1907-IV).

Republic of Buryatia, Law "On Public-Private Partnership in the Republic of Buryatia" (16 March 2012, #2625-IV).

Republic of Buryatia, Law "On Approving the Republican Target Programme "Development of Land Improvement Policy in the Republic of Buryatia in 2012-2014" (30 March 2012, #172).

Republic of Buryatia, Law "On the Republican Target Programme "Development of Water Management System in the Republic of Buryatia in 2013-2020" (15 October 2012, #605).

Republic of Buryatia, Law "On Approving the Republican Target Programme Development of Agricultural Sector and Rural Areas of the Republic of Buryatia" (28 February 2013, #102).

Republic of Buryatia, Law "On the Republican Target Programme "Protection of the Environment and Sustainable Use of Natural Resources" (30 May 2013, 261).

Republic of Buryatia, Law "On Approving the Republican Target Programme "Economic Development and Innovation-Driven Economy" (31 May 2013, #272).

Republic of Buryatia, Law "On Approving the Republican Target Programme "Development of Construction and Housing & Utilities Sector in the Republic of Buryatia" (2 August 2013, #424).

Republic of Buryatia, Law "On Approving the Investment Strategy of the Republic of Buryatia till 2020" (7 February 2014, #39).

Other official materials (authors of which are not indicated)

Explanatory Note to Draft Regulations on the Use of Water Resources of Irkutsk Water Storage Basins and Lake Baikal (2013), research work "*Refining the Draft Regulations on the Use of Water Resources of Water Storage Basins of the Angara HES Cascade (Irkutsk Water Storage Basin and Lake Baikal, and Bratsk and Ust-Ilimsk Water Storage Basins*)" http://pivr.enbvu.ru/pivr/pivr_irkutsk.zip.

Developing the mechanisms for implementation of a Target programme enabling the transition of the Republic of Buryatia to Sustainable Development for 2002-2010. Assessing the impact of "Baikal Factor", and developing the recommendations on how to finance environmental measures and compensate for extra costs associated with the Baikal Natural Area (2002), Scientific Report, Moscow.

Territorial Comprehensive Scheme of Environmental Protection of Lake Baikal Basin (1990).

Department of Federal Service for Control of Protection of Consumers and Human Welfare, Materials of Republican Inter-Agency Seminar "Protection of Water objects and Water Supply Sources" (28 November 2013).

Publications on International Practice in Water Recourses Management

Bongaerts, J.C. and A. Kraemer (1989), "Permits and effluent charges in the water pollution control policies of France, West Germany and the Netherlands", *Environmental Monitoring and Assessment,* May, Vol. 12/2, Springer, pp. 127-147.

Boyd, J. (2003), "The new face of the Clean Water Act: A critical review of the EPA's proposed TMDL rules", *RFF discussion paper,* No. 00-12, Resources for the Future, Washington, DC.

Buyuksagis, E. and W.H. van Boom (2013), "Strict liability in contemporary European codification: Torn between objects, activities and their risks", Vol. 44/2, Georgetown Journal of International Law, Georgetown University, Washington, DC., pp. 609-640.

Cowan, S. (1998), "Water pollution and abstraction and economic instruments", *Oxford Review of Economic Policy,* Vol. 14/4.

Demouliere, R., et al. (2010), *Public water supply and sanitation services in France,* third edition, FP2E and BIPE, Paris.

Denton, J.E. (2007), *A Review of the Potential Human and Environmental Health Impacts of Synthetic Motor Oils,* April, California Environmental Protection Agency, Office of Environmental Health Hazard Assessment, Sacramento, California.

Dinar, A. (ed.) (2000), *The Political Economy of Water Pricing Reforms.* World Bank, Washington, DC.

Environment Canada (2015), Used oil recycling program website, www.ec.gc.ca/gdd-mw/ (accessed 1 April 2015).

Ernst and Young (2013), *Water Resources at the Corporate Level. Moving from a Risk-based Approach to Active Management,* London.

European Federation of National Association of Water and Wastewater Services (2009), *EUREAU Statistics Overview on Water and Wastewater in Europe 2008. Country Profiles and European Statistics,* Brussels.

Government of the United Kingdom, Communities and Local Government (2006), *Planning Policy Statement 25: Development and Flood Risk,* London.

Government of the United States (1987), Water Quality Act.

Government of the United States (1972), Water Pollution Control Act.

Government of the United States (1972), Clean Water Act.

Hanley, N. et al. (2006), "Estimating the benefits of water quality improvements under the Water Framework Directive: are benefits transferable?" *European Review of Agricultural Economics*, Vol. 33/3, Oxford University Press, Oxford, pp. 391-413.

Heyes, A. (ed.) (2001), *The Law and Economics of the Environment,* Edward Elgar, Cheltenham, UK and Northampton, US.

Houck, O. (2002), *The Clean Water Act TMDL Program: Law, Policy, and Implementation,* Environmental Law Institute, Washington, DC.

IEEP et al. (2007), *Reforming Environmentally Harmful Subsidies.* Final report to the European Commission's DG Environment, 19 March, Institute for European Environmental Policy, London and Brussels.

International Water Association (2010), *International Statistics for Water Services. Information Every Water Manager Should Know About*, London.

Komives, K. et al. (2006), The distributional incidence of residential water and electricity subsidies, *Working Paper,* No. 3878, World Bank, Washington, DC.

Koundouri, P., B. Groom and O. Gonzalez Davila (2014), *Water Resources Management and Water Policy: Draft Policy Report to the OECD for the Lake Baikal Project,* London School of Economics and Political Science.

Koundouri, P. et al. (2013), "Introducing the case study, the Asopos River Basin in Greece", *DEOS Working Papers,* No. 1310, Athens University of Economics and Business, Athens.

Kraemer, R.A., E. Kampa and E. Interwies (2003), *The Role of Tradable Permits in Water Pollution Control*, Inter-American Development Bank, Washington, DC.

Kraemer, R.A., B. Pielen and A. Leipprand (2003), "Global review of economic instruments for water management in Latin America", *Working Paper for the Inter-American Development Bank. Regional Policy Dialogue, Environment Network, Meeting II: Application of Economic Instruments in Water and Solid Waste Management*, 25-26 February 2003, Washington, DC.

Martin-Ortega, J., R. Brouwer and J. Berbel (2009), *Economic analysis of spatial preferences heterogeneity of water quality,* presentation at the International Association of Agricultural Economists Conference, Beijing, 16-22 August.

Marques, R.C. (2010), *Regulation of Water and Wastewater Services. An International Comparison,* International Water Association Publishing, London.

OECD (2016), *Reforming Economic Instruments for Water Resources Management in Kyrgyzstan*, OECD Publishing, Paris. http://dx.doi.org/10.1787/9789264249363-en.

OECD EAP Task Force (2015), *Assessing and evaluating opportunities for (potentially) more efficient alternatives* (Interim Report #2), OECD, Paris, www.oecd.org/env/outreach/REPORT_1%20Economic%20Instruments%20for%20water%20management%20in%20the%20Republic%20of%20Buryatia.pdf.

OECD EAP Task Force (2014), *Review of the implementation of economic instruments for water management in the Republic of Buryatia* (Interim Report #1), OECD, Paris, www.oecd.org/env/outreach/REPORT_2%20Economic%20Instruments%20for%20water%20management%20in%20the%20Republic%20of%20Buryatia.pdf.

OECD EAP Task Force (2013a), *Economic Instruments for Water Resources Management in the Russian Federation,* OECD, Paris, www.oecd.org/env/outreach/EIs%20for%20WRM%20in%20Russia_English_Final%20web.pdf.

OECD EAP Task Force (2013b), *Improving the Use of Economic Instruments for Water Resources Management in Kyrgyzstan: the Case of Lake Issyk-Kul Basin,* OECD, Paris, www.oecd.org/environment/outreach/Kyrgyzstan_Eis%20for%20WRM_2nd%20edition_ENG%20web.pdf.

OECD EAP Task Force (2013c) Economic Instruments for Water Management in Russia: Legal and Regulatory Information, OECD, Paris, www.oecd.org/env/outreach/Info%20on%20Economic%20Instruments%20for%20Water%20Management%20in%20Russia.pdf.

OECD (2012a), *A Framework for Financing Water Resources Management,* OECD Publishing, Paris, http://dx.doi.org/10.1787/9789264179820-en.

OECD (2012b), *Overview of Key Methods Used to Identify and Quantify Environmentally-Harmful Subsidies with a Focus on the Energy Sector*: Draft report, ENV/EPOC/EAP(2012)2, https://www.oecd.org/env/outreach/EAP(2012)2_NP_Subsidies%20report_ENG.pdf.

OECD (2012c), *Refocusing Economic and Other Monetary Instruments for Greater Environmental Impact: How to Unblock Reform in Eastern Europe, Caucasus and Central Asia,* OECD Publishing, Paris, www.oecd.org/env/outreach/2012_EM_Refocusing%20Economic%20Instruments_ENG.pdf.

OECD (2010a), *Paying for Biodiversity. Enhancing the Cost-Effectiveness of Payments for Ecosystem Services,* OECD Publishing, Paris, http://dx.doi.org/10.1787/9789264090279-en.

OECD (2010b), *Pricing Water Resources and Water and Sanitation Services,* OECD Publishing, Paris, http://dx.doi.org/10.1787/9789264083608-en.

OECD (2009a), *Managing Water for All: An OECD Perspective on Pricing and Financing,* OECD Publishing, Paris, http://dx.doi.org/10.1787/9789264059498-en.

OECD (2009b), *Strategic Financial Planning for Water Supply and Sanitation.* A Report from the OECD Task Team on Sustainable Financing to Ensure Affordable Access to Water Supply and Sanitation, OECD Publishing, Paris, https://www.oecd.org/env/resources/43949580.pdf.

OECD (2009c), *Dealing with Post-Decentralisation Implications in the Water Supply and Sanitation sector. A Cross-Country Analysis,* OECD Publishing, Paris, www.oecd.org/env/outreach/44096445.pdf.

OECD (2007), *Instrument Mixes in Addressing Non-point Source Pollution,* OECD Papers, Special Issue on Environment, Volume 7(8), OECD Publishing, Paris, http://dx.doi.org/10.1787/oecd_papers-v7-art24-en.

OECD (2006), *Mechanisms for Managing Public Environmental Expenditures in Selected OECD Countries,* OECD Publishing, Paris, https://www.cbd.int/financial/expenditure/several-expmanage-oecd.pdf.

OECD (1978), *Recommendation of the OECD Council on Water Management Policies and Instruments* (C(78)4/FINAL), 5 April, OECD, Paris, http://olisweb.oecd.org/vgn-ext-templating/C(90)177-FINAL-ENG.pdf?docId=IMP19901146ENG&date=1144915088000&documentId=541926&organisationId=1&fileName=IMP19901146ENG.pdf.

Rosenberger, R.S. and J.B. Loomis (2000), "Using meta-analysis for benefit transfer: In-sample convergent validity tests of an outdoor recreation database", *Water Resources Research,* Vol. 36/4, AGU Wiley, pp. 1097-1107.

Shapkhaev, S.G. (2013), *Accounting of environmental and climatic factors for regulation of water flow regime of Lake Baikal at the Angara and Yenisei HES cascades* // Rivers of Siberia and Far East: Proceedings of VIII International Research and Practice Conference, Irkutsk: IROO "Baikal Environmental Wave", pp. 19-22.

Somanathan, J.E. and T. Sterner (2004), "Environmental policy instruments and institutions in developing countries", *Working Paper Series,* Initiative for Policy Dialogue, Columbia University, New York.

Stephenson, J. (2012), "Business, biodiversity and ecosystem services. Policy priorities for engaging business to improve the health of ecosystems and conserve biodiversity", presentation at the 28th roundtable on sustainable development, Hyderabad, 16 October 2012.

Sterner, T. (2003), *Policy Instruments for Environmental and Natural Resources Management,* Resources for the Future Press, Washington, DC.

Strosser, P. (2010), *Economic instruments for mobilising financial resources for supporting IWRM; Additional information and illustrations for the OECD initiative*, Acteon-Environment, OECD Publishing, Paris.

Swedish Water and Wastewater Association (2000), *Facts on Water Supply and Sanitation in Sweden,* Stockholm.

UNESCO (2012), *Managing Water under Uncertainty and Risk: UN World Water Development Report*, Vol. 1/4, Geneva.

United Cities and Local Government (2010), *Global Observatory on Local Democracy and Decentralisation Third Report*: *Basic Services for All in an Urbanizing World*, Jakarta.

United Nations University (2006), *Water-Related Risk Management in Urban Agglomerations*, Institute for Environment and Human Security, Tokyo.

US EPA (2014), *Utilizing SRF Funding for Green Infrastructure Projects,* Environmental Protection Agency, Washington, DC.

US EPA (2012), *Safe and Sustainable Water Resources, Strategic Research Action Plan, 2012-2016*, Environmental Protection Agency, Washington, DC.

US EPA (2008), *Pawtucket, Rhode Island: A\Drinking Water State Revolving Fund Success Story,* September, Environmental Protection Agency, Washington, DC.

US EPA (2008), "Clean Water Financing", 1 December, Environmental Protection Agency, Washington, DC.

US EPA (1986), Toxic Release Inventory (TRI), emerged from the Emergency Planning and Community Right to Know Act of 1986, Environmental Protection Agency, Washington, DC.

US EPA-Philadelphia Green Cities/Clean Water Partnership (2012), website, www.phillywatersheds.org/.

Whelan, T. (1991), *Nature Tourism,* Island Press, Washington, DC.

Wunder, S. (2005), "Payment for environmental services, some nuts and bolts, *Occasional paper,* No. 42, Center for International Forestry Research, Bogor, Indonesia.

Publications in Russian

Bobylev, S.N. and V.M. Zakharov (2009), *Ecosystem Services and the Economy,* Institute for Sustainable Development, Moscow.

Ecotourism on the Way to Russia (2002), Principles, recommendations, Russian and international practice, World Wide Fund For Nature.

Environmental and Information Center "Zapovedniki" (2011), *Payments for Ecosystem Service: Theory, Methodology, and International Practice.*

Ivanov, V.A. (2013), *International Practice in Management of Water Supply and Sanitation Sector,* Guidance Manual, http://elibrary.udsu.ru/xmlui/handle/123456789/10934.

Other sources

Baikal Institute of Natural Management (2003), *Managing the Collection, Processing and Summarisation of Environmental and Economic Information in the Republic of Buryatia Scientific Report,* Ulan Ude, Siberian Branch of the Russian Academy of Sciences.

Bobovich, B.B. (1999), *Recycling of Industrial Waste,* Textbook for Institutions of Higher Education, "SP Intermet Engineering", Moscow.

Ekonimika (1996), "Model technique for determining the economic efficiency of environmental measures and assessing the economic damage caused by pollution of the environment to the national economy", Moscow.

GEF and UNDP (2014), *Analysis of the current cost control system and incentives to economic efficiency and enhancing the performance of water management organisations in Russia's part of Lake Baikal basin as it relates to infrastructure of irrigation, water supply and sanitation. Developing the proposals on how to streamline the system of cost control and strengthen the incentive in the foregoing sectors,* Project Report under the "Baikal project", Ulan Ude, Global Environment Facility and United Nations Development Programme, Washington, DC.

Government of the Russian Federation, Ministry of Natural Resources and Environmental Protection (2007, 2008, 2009, 2010, 2011, 2012), *"On the State of Environment and Environmental Protection in the Republic of Buryatia",* http://minpriroda-rb.ru/activity/index.php?section_ID=921.

Government of the Russian Federation, Ministry of Natural Resources and Environmental Protection *"On the State of Lake Baikal and Environmental Protection Measures"* (2005, 2006, 2007, 2008, 2009, 2010, 2011, 2012), www.mnr.gov.ru/regulatory/list.php?part=1258.

Government of the Russian Federation (1996, 1997, 1998, 2001, 2002, 2003), *Problems of Environmental Protection of Lake Baikal and Environmental Management in Baikal Region, Annual Report on Lake Baikal,* Government Commission, Moscow.

International Standards of Financial Reporting (2013), *State Subsidies Accounting and Disclosure of Information about State Support* (ed. 2 April 2013).

Lapusta M.G. and P.S. Nikolskiy (eds.) (2002), *Modern Financial Credit Dictionary*, INFRA-M, Moscow.

Liborakina M.I. and S.B. Sivaev (2004), *Local Self-Governance and Reforming of Housing and Utilities Sector,* Obshchestvenniye Nauki I Sovremennost, #3, 2004.

Methodological Analysis of Rental Payments in Water Management Sector (2004), Ulan Ude.

Protasov, V.F. (2001), *Ecology, Health, and Protection of the Environment in Russia*, Moscow.

Protasov, V.F. and A.V. Molchanov (1995), *Ecology, Health, and Environmental Management I Russia*, Finansy i Statistika, Moscow.

Reimers, N.F. (1990), *Environmental Management: Dictionary and Reference Guide*, Mysl, Moscow.

Republic of Buryatia (2013), *Environmental Protection in the Republic of Buryatia, Statistics Digest*, No. 06-07-08, Goskomstat of the Republic of Buryatia, Ulan Ude Republic of Buryatia (2012, 2013), Buryatia in Figures, Statistics Digest, State Statistics Service of the Republic of Buryatia, Ulan Ude.

Republic of Buryatia (2003), Eighty Years to Buryatia, Statistics Digest, State Statistics Service of the Republic of Buryatia, Ulan Ude.

Republic of Buryatia, Data gathered according to the form of statistical accounting #1-NM "Report on Assessment and Collection of Taxes, Charges, and Other Compulsory Payments to the Budget of the RF" and #5-VN"On a Tax Base and Tax Structure of Water Tax" in the Republic of Buryatia, Federal Tax Service – www.nalog.ru/opendata/.

Republic of Buryatia, Data gathered according to the form of federal statistical accounting #1-zhilfond/housing stock, #1-vodoprovod/water supply, # 1-kanalizatzia (sewerage), #1-KKh, #22-ZhKKh (consolidated), #22-ZhKKh (subsidies) for the Republic of Buryatia in 2008-2012, Rosstat.

Rosstat (2013), *Regions of Russia, Socio-Economic Indicators (2013),* Statistics Digest, Moscow.

Russian and German Bureau of Environmental Information (2013), *Sustainable Development in Russia*, Berlin-St. Petersburg.

Sivaev S., L. Pertzov and A. Rodionov (2014), *Provision of Public Services at the Local Level in Russia: Stages of Development and the Current State,* Institute of Urban Economics, Moscow.

Shapkhaev, S.G. (2013), *Accounting of Environmental and Climatic Factors in the Context of Regulation of Water Flows of Lake Baikal by the Angara and Yenisei HES Cascades, Rivers of Siberia and Far East,* Materials of the VIII International Environmental Science and Applied Research Conference, IROO "Baikal Environmental Wave", Irkutsk.

Shevchuk, A. (2013), *Water Resources Management, Aquatic Ecology Problems*, in a digest "Sustainable Development in Russia", Russian and German Bureau of Environmental Information, Berlin-St. Petersburg.

SNiS (2003), "Technical Protection of Territories, Buildings, and Facilities from Hazardous Geological Processes, General Provisions", 22 February 2003.

Tulokhonov, A.K. (2010), *Baikal Problem: History and Documents*, EKOS, Ulan Ude.

Vikulov, V.Y. (1982), *Regime of Special Management of Environmental Resources: Case Study of Lake Baikal,* Nauka, Novosibirsk.

Zhigalov D.V. and L.V. Pertzov (2011), *Financial Principles of Local Self Governance: Outcomes of the 2000s*, Budget #7, 2011.

Note

1. The legal acts listed below are available at the official web site of the federal government www.gov.ru.

Annex B

Essential research efforts required for implementation of the recommendations

No.	Subject of research	Use of research findings
1	Assessing the impact of various economic activities on the state of biosphere of the BNA	Mitigation of administrative bans along with a wider use of economic instruments for managing economic activities in the Central Environmental Zone of the BNA (2.3.3)
2	Evaluating the natural capital of the ecosystem in the BNA; elaborating a concept of development of environment-oriented activities, development and introduction of payment for ecosystem services	1. Promotion of charging for ecosystem services (2.3.5). 2. Expanding state support to environment-oriented activities for enhancement of capitalisation of the BNA (2.3.4)
3	Developing methodology for assessing and estimating damage from negative impact of hydro-energy industry on the ecosystem of Lake Baikal, the economy and population of the coastal areas; streamlining the approaches to determining the amount and fair redistribution of hydro-energy rent	Redistribution of hydro-energy rent and introduction of a compensation mechanism for damage to the ecosystem of Lake Baikal and the economy of the coastal areas by the Angara HES cascade (2.3.6)
4	Developing a procedural framework for compulsory disclosure of environmental information by enterprises located in the BNA	Scientific and regulatory support in the context of introducing the system of compulsory disclosure of environmental information in the BNA, and, in the long run, in other territories of environmental significance located in the RF (2.1.4)
5	Developing a technique for determining the volumes of the maximum allowable aggregate daily discharge of key polluting substances, as well as limits of discharges of certain polluting substances into water objects	Setting limits of discharges of certain polluting substances into water objects and eventual development of a market for pollution quotas (2.2.3)
6	Introducing additional multiplying factors to be applied to basic rates of charges for polluting effluents in the BNA, differentiated according to environmental zones and with due account for environmental capacity of territories; revising the limits of the maximum allowable discharges for centralised sanitation systems and their users	Improving the procedures of charging and collection of payments for negative impact on the environment (2.2.2)
7	Detecting the impact of toxic agrochemicals and synthetic detergents on Lake Baikal; identifying the list of substances the use of which is entirely prohibited in the BNA, and the list of substances for whose use a charge (tax) is levied, determining the rate of a charge (tax) according to types of subsidies	Prohibiting the use of the most toxic agrochemicals in the RB and levying a tax (charge) on toxic agrichemicals (pesticides, herbicides, etc.) and synthetic detergents (2.2.4)
8	Developing a package of standard technical solutions designed to enable the achievement of wastewater treatment standards	Facilitating state support regarding the implementation of wastewater treatment technologies to enable the attainment of standards for quality of water objects within the BNA (2.5.3)

No.	Subject of research	Use of research findings
9	Refining "The Regulations on the Use of Water Resources of Lake Baikal and Water Storage Reservoirs of the Angara HES Cascade (and its interrelationship with similar regulations for Yenisei HES cascade) Developing a system of monitoring for response of water and coastal ecosystems to changes in water levels in Lake Baikal, as a result of extreme situations, and using the monitoring results for adjusting the above regulations	Facilitating efforts to ensure that water-level fluctuations of Lake Baikal are close to their multi-year natural values (2.3.7)
10	Creating a system of classification of territories of the RB prone to water-related hazards according to a degree of probability of occurrence of emergency situations associated with water resources	Introduction of economic mechanisms for management of risks associated with water-related hazards, and of a mechanism of differentiation of land tax rates and property tax rates (as these relate to immovable property) (2.6.2-2.6.3.)
11	Developing a technique for estimating the probability of risks for water resources, and the related ecosystems, and assessing the impact of risks	Introduction of economic mechanisms for management of risks for water resources, and the related ecosystems, and, in that regard, development of compulsory insurance of non-critical risks (2.6.4)
12	Researching into the impact of permafrost on the level of ground water pollution	Development of proposals on protection of ground water from pollution taking into account the impact of permafrost (2.3.3)

Annex C

Agendas of meetings of Inter-Agency Co-ordinating Group set up to supervise implementation of the project

First meeting of Inter-agency Co-ordinating Group

on implementation of the OECD project "Facilitating the Development of Economic Instruments for Management of Water Resources in the Republic of Buryatia (Lake Baikal basin)"

Ulan Ude, the Republic of Buryatia, 17 January 2014

10.45 - 11.00	**Registration of participants**
11.00 - 13.00	**Opening ceremony** 1. Welcome remarks by representatives of state authorities of the Republic of Buryatia: – *Angayev B.D., Minister of Natural Resources of the Republic of Buryatia* – *Smolin V.V., Deputy Minister of Economics of the Republic of Buryatia* 2. Presentation of tasks and expected outcomes of the project *Martoussevitch A.P., Senior Project Manager, Organisation for Economic Co-operation and Development (OECD)* 3. Major approaches to project implementation, organising for collection of necessary information, work stages implementation – *Sivaev S.B., Pertzov L.V., the Institute for Urban Economics (IUE)* 4. Discussion and designing of the project action plan 5. Closing of the Meeting

Second meeting of Inter-Agency Co-ordinating Group

on implementation of the OECD project "Facilitating the Development of Economic Instruments for Management of Water Resources in the Republic of Buryatia (Lake Baikal basin)"

Ulan Ude, the Republic of Buryatia, 4 July 2014

8:45 a.m.- 9 a.m.	**Registration of participants**
9 a.m.– 9:20 a.m.	**Opening of the Meeting** Welcome remarks: – *Tulukhonov A.K., member of the Council of Federation of the Federal Assembly of the Republic of Buryatia* – *Lbov A.V., First Deputy Minister of Natural Resources of the Republic of Buryatia* – *Martoussevitch A.P., Senior Project Manager, Organisation for Economic Co-operation and Development (OECD)* Presentation of participants and the agenda of the meeting
9:20 a.m.- 10:30 a.m.	**Session 1** **Presentation of Report "Analysis of the Use of Economic Instruments for Management of Water Resources in the Republic of Buryatia"** *Moderator: Martoussevitch A.P.* Presentation of the Report (30 minutes): *Pertzov L.V., the IUE* *RodionovA.Yu., the IUE* *Bardakhanova T.B., Baikal Institute of Nature Management, Siberian Branch of the Russian Academy of Sciences* Discussion
10:30 a.m.- 10:50 a.m.	**Coffee Break**
10:50 a.m.- 11:50 a.m.	**Session 2** **International practice in water resources management that could be used in the Republic of Buryatia** *Moderator: Pertzov L.V.* Presentation of international practice in water resources management, *Martoussevitch A.P.*(25 minutes) Discussion
11:50 a.m.- 1 p.m.	**Session 3** **Priority areas for improvement of economic instruments for water resources management in the Republic of Buryatia** *Moderator: Lbov A.V.* Presentation of draft recommendations, *Pertzov L.V.*(20 minutes) Discussion
1 p.m.- 1:15 p.m.	Closing of the Meeting

Third meeting of Inter-Agency Co-ordinating Group

on implementation of the OECD project "Facilitating the Development of Economic Instruments for Management of Water Resources in the Republic of Buryatia (Lake Baikal basin)"

Ulan Ude, the Republic of Buryatia, 19 December 2014

9:45 a.m.- 10 a.m.	**Registration of participants**
10 a.m.- 10:20 a.m.	**Opening of the Meeting** Welcome remarks: – *Lbov A.V., First Deputy Minister of Natural Resources of the Republic of Buryatia* – *Martoussevitch A.P., Senior Project Manager, Organisation for Economic Co-operation and Development (OECD)* Presentation of participants and agenda of the meeting
10:20 a.m.- 12 p.m.	**Session 1** **Recommendations on improving water resources management in the Republic of Buryatia** Presentation of recommendations (30 minutes): *Pertzov L.V., the IUE* Discussion *Moderator: Martoussevitch A.P*
12 p.m.- 12:45 p.m.	**Session 2** **Key actions advisable for implementation of the presented recommendations** Discussion *Moderator: Lbov A.V.*
12:45 p.m.- 13:00 p.m.	Closing of the Meeting
1 p.m.- 2 p.m.	**Coffee**

Annex D

Glossary

- **Capitalisation of BNA** is understood as transformation of natural resources (including water and biodiversity), ecosystem services and aesthetic value of nature and landscapes located in the BNA into economic assets able to generate revenues and other economic benefits, and assigning monetary value to the assets, economic activities and businesses operating on the BNA territory. It could be assigned by market (if it exists) or through a dedicated monetary evaluation by qualified experts.
- "***Implementability***" (of a proposed measure) – high-medium-low, is a qualitative characteristic of the degree of expected political support or resistance to the proposed measure, and of its financial and technical feasibility, taking into account present and future resource constraints (that is, how easy or difficult it would be to implement the measure).
- **Water infrastructure** is a set of facilities related to the use of water resources and objects and/or prevention and elimination of the negative impact of water-related hazards, including hydro-technical structures, water supply and sanitation (WSS) systems, water treatment facilities, collection and removal of storm water infrastructure, irrigation systems and buildings and structures used for monitoring and studying water objects.
- **Water management** includes management of water resources and of water infrastructure, as well as management of water-related risks.
- **Water object** is a natural or artificial water reservoir, waterway, ground water deposit or other object, permanent or temporary mass of water characterised by temporal changes in the water table level, consumption and volume of water.
- **Water resources** are freshwater, brackish water and saltwater found in surface and underground water objects that are used or may be used.
- **Water sector** is a set of water infrastructure institutions and types of activity related to the use, research and protection of water resources and water objects, as well as the prevention and elimination of the negative impact of water-related hazards.

ORGANISATION FOR ECONOMIC CO-OPERATION AND DEVELOPMENT

The OECD is a unique forum where governments work together to address the economic, social and environmental challenges of globalisation. The OECD is also at the forefront of efforts to understand and to help governments respond to new developments and concerns, such as corporate governance, the information economy and the challenges of an ageing population. The Organisation provides a setting where governments can compare policy experiences, seek answers to common problems, identify good practice and work to co-ordinate domestic and international policies.

The OECD member countries are: Australia, Austria, Belgium, Canada, Chile, the Czech Republic, Denmark, Estonia, Finland, France, Germany, Greece, Hungary, Iceland, Ireland, Israel, Italy, Japan, Korea, Latvia, Luxembourg, Mexico, the Netherlands, New Zealand, Norway, Poland, Portugal, the Slovak Republic, Slovenia, Spain, Sweden, Switzerland, Turkey, the United Kingdom and the United States. The European Union takes part in the work of the OECD.

OECD Publishing disseminates widely the results of the Organisation's statistics gathering and research on economic, social and environmental issues, as well as the conventions, guidelines and standards agreed by its members.

OECD PUBLISHING, 2, rue André-Pascal, 75775 PARIS CEDEX 16
(97 2016 23 1 P) ISBN 978-92-64-26629-2 – 2016

www.ingramcontent.com/pod-product-compliance
Ingram Content Group UK Ltd.
Pitfield, Milton Keynes, MK11 3LW, UK
UKHW051505290926
15471UKWH00008B/1428

9 789264 266292